I Was Born There,
I Was Born Here

By the same author

Prose
I Saw Ramallah

Poetry
A Small Sun
Midnight and Other Poems

I Was Born There, I Was Born Here

Mourid Barghouti

Translated from the Arabic by
Humphrey Davies

Walker & Company
New York

Copyright © 2011 by Mourid Barghouti
English translation copyright © 2011 by Humphrey Davies
Foreword copyright © 2011 by John Berger

The poems on pages vii, 113, 142–3, 166, 192, and 193–4 appeared in
Midnight and Other Poems by Mourid Barghouti (trans. Radwa Ashour),
published by Arc Publications. Reproduced by permission.

Published by Walker Publishing Company, Inc., New York
A Division of Bloomsbury Publishing

All papers used by Walker & Company are natural, recyclable products
made from wood grown in well-managed forests. The manufacturing processes conform to
the environmental regulations of the country of origin.

This book has been selected to receive financial assistance from English PEN's Writers in
Translation program supported by Bloomberg. English PEN exists to promote literature and its
understanding, uphold writers' freedoms around the world, campaign against the persecution and
imprisonment of writers for stating their views, and promote the friendly cooperation of writers
and free exchange of ideas.

Recommended by pen

LIBRARY OF CONGRESS CATALOGING-IN-PUBLICATION DATA

Barghuthi, Murid.
[Wulidtu hunak, wulidtu huna. English]
I was born there, I was born here / Mourid Barghouti ; translated from the Arabic by Humphrey Davies.
p. cm.
Short stories. Translated from Arabic.
ISBN 978-0-8027-7997-7
I. Davies, Humphrey T. (Humphrey Taman) II. Title.
PJ7816.A682W8513 2011
892.7'36—dc23
2011040852

Visit Walker & Company's Web site at www.walkerbooks.com

First published in Arabic in 2009 by Riad El-Rayyes Books as *Wulidtu hunak, wulidtu huna*
Protected under the Berne Convention

First U.S. edition 2012

1 3 5 7 9 10 8 6 4 2

Typeset by Adam el Sehemy
Printed in the U.S.A. by Quad/Graphics, Fairfield, Pennsylvania

For Radwa Ashour

Forgive me if what has seemed little to you, to me is all.

—José Saramago

Contents

'Come Closer', Foreword *by John Berger*   xi

1 The Driver Mahmoud   1
2 Father and Son   31
3 The Yasmin Building   53
4 I Was Born There, I Was Born Here   79
5 The Identity Card   107
6 The Ambulance   115
7 Saramago   137
8 The Alhambra   159
9 Things One Would Never Think Of   173
10 The Dawn Visitor   195
11 An Ending Leading to the Beginning?   211

Glossary   215

Come Closer

Foreword by John Berger

This book, with its fury and tenderness, its close observation and cosmic metaphors, is wild. Reading it, you follow graphically the experience of the Palestinian people during the last sixty years, and, at the same time, you partake of some of the most ancient recourses of the human imagination when faced with collective suffering and humiliation.

It has been written by the distinguished poet Mourid Barghouti, who is also the father of an honoured poet, Tamim Barghouti. It's a book that begs for an answer to the question: why write poetry? And, in begging, it gives its own lacerating, literal and sometimes lyrical answer.

I've read no other book in which poetry is so interleaved with the problems and shit (such as identity cards) of daily life, or in which a working poet—either the father or son—is felt to be so close to those for whom their poetry speaks. It comes from the heart of an endless tragedy where jokes are one of the principal means of survival. It redefines in such conditions what is "normal".

It's also fine to die in our beds
on a clean pillow
and among our friends.
It's fine to die, once,
our hands crossed on our chests
empty and pale
with no scratches, no chains, no banners,
no petitions.
It's fine to have an undusty death,
no holes in our shirts,
and no evidence in our ribs.
It's fine to die
with a white pillow, not the pavement, under our cheeks....

What has happened and is happening to the land of Palestine and its people is unclassifiable. None of the historical terms such as colonization, annexation, invasion or elimination are precise enough. The word 'Occupation', which is generally used, has been given a new vast meaning and this book spells out that meaning and the extension of what it means.

Perhaps it is for this reason that the book itself is unclassifiable. It's a book of heartrending stories, a book about poetics, a personal memoir, the history of a family, a journal of confessions, an uncompromising political tract attacking the state of Israel, the corruption of the so-called Palestinian Authority, and the self-serving dictatorships of the surrounding Arab countries. It is also a book of love—love for all those who, although powerless, somehow continue to live with dignity. With courage, too. Yet dignity offers not only an example, but also a shelter. These pages demonstrate how it does so.

The reader is brought face to face (like people come close together in a very small shelter) with what is happening in Palestine today (every day), which is inseparable from what happened yesterday and what people fear will happen tomorrow. The media never refer to what you discover here. Place names such as Jenin, al-Khalil, Rafah, Hebron and Qalandya become dense with experience.

This, however, is only part of what the book offers. There is something else. Mourid Barghouti's form of narrative insists that lived moments when they are momentous contain something that can be considered eternal, and that such moments, however brief and trivial they may appear to a third eye, join together and form a necklace called a lifetime. Living as we do in a consumerist culture, which recognizes only the latest and the instantaneous, we badly need this reminder. Thank you, Mourid.

I Was Born There,
I Was Born Here

The Driver Mahmoud

Here we are, safely arrived in Jericho, as he promised. I still can't believe we made it. Maybe it was luck, or the cell phones, or the wiliness of the villagers and shepherds, or maybe—most likely—fate hasn't made up its mind yet to let Palestinians die in road accidents. I think most, though, about our driver, Mahmoud.

I stand waiting for him in the hotel porch in Ramallah. He arrives more or less on time. This is nothing unusual for Darwish Tours, who are known for their punctuality. He leaves the taxi's engine running, steps down into the light rain, and comes toward me.

"Mr. Barghouti?"

He picks up my small suitcase (my suitcase is always small here because of the checkpoints) and hurriedly creates a space for it in the trunk. It's good that he doesn't lift it up onto the roof of the taxi along with the other luggage and good that he's picked up the six other passengers first so that we won't waste time searching for their addresses among the hills and valleys of Ramallah. I take my place in the yellow taxi and tell myself it's a good start to the day.

He sets off for Jericho without uttering a word, like someone hiding a secret and waiting for the right moment to tell it. Clearly he's decided to avoid the Qalandya checkpoint. The windshield wipers are no good at removing the imprint of the fog, which has taken on the color of zinc, and are losing their race with the rain, which is getting harder. The vehicles in the street are few, the pedestrians fewer.

We leave the confines of Ramallah.

Everything appears normal until he gets a call on his cell phone. He finishes it in seconds and increases speed noticeably. After a few kilometers, he leaves the main road and enters a village that I'm seeing for the first time and whose name I don't know but am too embarrassed to ask. Its one narrow street curves, then twists and turns among the houses before we leave it once more for the paved highway.

"Good morning, everyone. My name is Mahmoud and this is today's last taxi for the bridge. Israel has informed foreign diplomats the attack will take place tonight or tomorrow and told them to get out of harm's way. All the bastards care about is the foreigners; we're not human. The army's on alert, the roads are closed, and there are flying checkpoints everywhere. The weather as you can see is bad but we'll definitely make it to the bridge, with God's help. Coffee? Pour a cup for everyone, Hajj—'the great man lives to serve his people,' as they say. Please, have some coffee."

The passengers don't appear particularly upset at the news of the impending attack announced by Mahmoud. In fact, the fat passenger sitting in front of me in the middle seat comments sarcastically: "As if the film needed more action! Every day they kill us retail and once in a while they get the urge to kill us wholesale. Big deal! They've launched a hundred attacks before and it's done them no good. They're really stuck. Like they say, 'Stupidity is trying what's already been tried and expecting different results.' The only thing they're good at is shooting and killing. Each time they attack, go bam-bam-bam, drop bombs from airplanes, and leave. What's the point?"

"It's a farce!" says his neighbor. "When you see them invading our villages and camps, you'd think they were off to conquer China, though they could arrest any of us any time, including Yasser Arafat, or expel him from the country, or imprison him, or kill him, without tanks or armored vehicles or F-16s. Who'd stop them?"

He falls silent for a moment. Then he says, as though to himself, "Anyway, their project isn't going well, I can tell you. An Israeli state at our expense isn't working out for them. How do they think they're going to get away from us? Do they suppose they can kill us all? The project's dragged them into a mess, there's no end in sight, and they know that each year gets them in deeper. You're right, they're really stuck."

I, who for long years have been away from these people, from my countrymen and the details of their daily lives, cannot make light of the plans of a terrifying individual such as Sharon to invade our cities and our villages. To them, though—the inhabitants of these same cities and villages, who haven't been distanced by successive exiles— everything has become food for jokes. Is it familiarity or stoicism? Is it a confidence built up by a culture of living inside the details or a sign of the resistance they embody simply by remaining in place?

I decide to convince myself too that everything's normal. I prefer not to show my anxiety over what the engineer of the Sabra and Shatila massacre will do tomorrow, or the day after, when he unleashes his tanks and massed troops—themselves armored like tanks—onto our streets. I think to myself, If only our leadership, petrified of Israel as it is, could grasp the truth of Israel's dilemma the way these passengers have.

The driver produces from beneath his feet a thermos of coffee, which he hands to the old man seated next to him, supplying him at the same time with a stack of small plastic cups.

As the first cup is poured, the smell of the coffee enters into a stealthy race with that of the cardamom. The cardamom wins, of course.

"Lord, bring it all down on Sharon's head! Have some coffee, son, daughter. It's very hot. Give some to the lady. Please, go ahead," says the Hajj.

The cup reaches me via the hand of the girl sitting in front of me in the middle seat. I take it gingerly, look at it, raise it to my lips, and take a first sip.

Now *this* is coffee. It may not have the elegant cup that would make it some other kind of coffee, but it's a *perfectly timed* cup of coffee. People can't agree on where coffee's secret lies: opinions range from the smell, the color, the taste, the consistency, the blend, the cardamom, the roast, to the shape of the cup and a number of other things. For me, it's the timing. The great thing about a perfectly timed cup of coffee is that it's in your hand the instant you crave it. One of life's most exquisite moments is that in which a small luxury becomes a necessity. And someone has to present the coffee to you, because coffee is like roses: someone else has to present you with roses, you can't present them to yourself. And if you do make the coffee yourself, it's because at that moment you're on your own, with no lover or anyone else to think of, a stranger in your own home. If it's by choice, then you're paying the price of your freedom; if it's by necessity, you need to hear the doorbell ring. Its colors are also tastes and flavors—the blond and the dark, the full roast and the medium—so it acquires its different meanings from the expression on the face of the one who offers it to you and the circumstances in which they offer it. Coffee the first time you meet someone is different from coffee to make peace after a spat, which is different from coffee that the guest refuses to drink until a demand is met. Writing coffee is different from reading coffee, and coffee on a journey from coffee at home. Coffee in a hotel is different from coffee in your house, and coffee made on an open hearth from that made in a machine, while coffee from a cheerful face in a café is different from coffee from a sullen, gloomy face. And if the 'dawn visitor' tells you, with official courtesy and a weapon-bearing smile, as he tears you from your family and leads you away, "We'd like you to have a coffee at our place," it's a form of kidnapping, or murder; foolish is the man who trusts the government's coffee. Again, coffee at a wedding is different from coffee at a wake, where 'coffee' loses all meaning and is handed round to the miserable company by an equally miserable 'waiter,' who doesn't know his guests and doesn't ask them how they like it. There, the waiter's no waiter and the coffee's no coffee, its cup cone-shaped and handleless, its timing and its flavor not of your choosing—the last thing you could care about on such a day, as though it had lost its very name forever.

This morning, however, Mahmoud's offer of coffee comes at the perfect time and, along with the lively rain outside, sends a joy through my veins that is at odds with the bad news.

"But no smoking, if you'd be so kind. We'll be there in an hour," says the Hajj.

"What do you mean, an hour, Hajj?" says another. "Make that two, three hours . . . four. You heard what the man said: we may get there and we may not."

Mahmoud smiles and corrects him confidently: "I said we *will* get there."

A boy in his early twenties, with a broad forehead, a puzzling mole on his right cheek that I can't make up my mind about, and small eyes that combine blackness and brightness; a boy confident as a new lamp, alert as a lawyer seized by a sudden idea, his voice commanding but not rough. Even in his winter clothes, he looks skinny. His expression is serious but relaxed and relaxing, assured and reassuring. Though young, he drives the car with an old hand's seemingly careless care.

Between me and the fully veiled lady in the rear seat sits a sad young man who I tell myself must have a story. Everyone in this world has a story and since I hate it when anyone asks me, "What's wrong?" I don't ask him why he's sad. During a passing glance in his direction, however, I find him smiling mischievously and his eyes direct me to a strange scene. The lady is lifting the end of her veil with her left hand and holding it out in front, creating a long trunk of thick black cloth with a secret passage beneath it down which her right hand brings the cup of coffee to her lips with a careful speed that speaks of long experience. Then she lowers the cloth again, closing off the alimentary tunnel as quickly as she opened it and before anyone can catch a glimpse of what it is she's trying to conceal. I pretend not to notice, even though the scene is totally new to me, as during my years abroad I have never seen a fully veiled woman taking food or drink in public. I do, however, steal another look and catch her reopening the obligatory tunnel, inserting the cup of coffee into it with the same studied care, and taking another sip. She appears to regard the procedure as perfectly normal.

In the three middle seats are two men and a young woman, of whom all I can see are her hair, which is tied in a pony tail, and her small ears, which are without earrings (I think of my wonderful friend 'Ali al-Shawk and his mixture of astonishment and disapproval at women's need to dangle things from their ears). One of the men must be very short, as his kufiya and the cord that keeps it in place are only just visible above the back of the seat, so that I can imagine but not see him. The other is the fat man with the cheerful air. Before offering the coffee to his nearly invisible neighbor, he says playfully to Mahmoud, "My friend's from al-Khalil. Should I give him coffee or better not risk it?"

We all laugh. Even the veiled lady laughs out loud.

If he's opened the door to jokes against people from al-Khalil, I think to myself, it'll never get shut again.

Mahmoud wants to provoke further jokes to lighten the mood, and says with false innocence, "What's wrong with people from al-Khalil?"

Then he adds, imitating an Egyptian accent, "The Khalilis are great guys and al-Khalil's a real man's town, swear to God."

"Are you Khalili, Mahmoud my friend?"

"I used to be but I got treatment."

The man from al-Khalil laughs loudly and we laugh along with him once more.

Mahmoud adds, seriously this time, "I'm from al-Am'ari Camp."

"An honor. Good people."

Egyptians make jokes about Upper Egyptians, Syrians about the people of Homs, Jordanians about people from Tafileh, and Lebanese about 'Abu al-'Abid,' the theme in all cases being their naïveté or empty bragging. The Palestinians make jokes about the people of al-Khalil, the point being their hard-headedness. Generally, people ask about the latest joke, but Mahmoud, in a strange departure from tradition, asks the passenger from al-Khalil what was the first joke ever made about the people of his town. The man, sunk in his seat, says, "I don't really know, but my grandfather used to tell the story of a man from al-Khalil who falls from the seventh story and doesn't die but gets up again, sound as a bell. Someone says to him, 'Here's a hundred lira to do it again,' but the man refuses, saying, 'How can I be sure I'll land on my head next time?'"

Then Mahmoud asks, "And what's the worst? I mean the joke they really can't stand."

"When the settler Baruch Goldstein opened fire on the worshipers in the Sanctuary of Ibrahim in al-Khalil and killed twenty-nine of them, someone said a few days after the massacre, 'There would have been more casualties if Baruch hadn't fired at their heads.'"

I haven't heard the joke before, even though the massacre at the Sanctuary of Ibrahim took place in 1994. I don't laugh. There have been so many massacres that they've become material for their victims' jokes. In this uneven conflict with the Occupation, which bears the most modern weapons of the age, the unarmed Palestinian hates to be an object of pity. He arms himself with laughter and irony, even at his own expense, and by making fun of his repeated tragedies under this seemingly endless Occupation. People no longer complain to one another about the prisons, the curfews, the repeated closures and invasions. I don't know whether getting used to these atrocities is a weakness or a strength. If getting used to oppression is a sign of the slave, one confident of the justice of his cause may find in it a way of tamping down his anger and stoking the elements of a hidden strength. One sign of strength in the oppressed is the ability to mock the powerful, and an unspoken readiness to respond in time, however distant that time may be. While waiting, the oppressed exercise their senses to the full in their lust for life.

It would be a big lie to claim that the oppressed do nothing with their lives and in their lives but resist oppression.

The oppressed cling to any of life's joys that may be granted them, no matter how small. They let no opportunity for love, good cheer, or the pleasures of the body or soul escape them.

The oppressed strive to fulfil desires both obscure and obvious, no matter how rarely the chances come and no matter how difficult they are to realize.

I was delighted by a truly lovely story related to me by a young poet I'd met on an earlier visit, at the Shorouk Bookstore in Ramallah. He told me how happy he'd been when the loudspeakers unexpectedly announced the Israeli army's complete closure of the town and how grateful he was in his heart to the army because the closure and the curfew would oblige the girl whom he loved, a relative of his who was visiting his family, to spend the whole night in their house, without fear of reproach from her parents. The next day, when the curfew was lifted and the checkpoints opened, the village, of course, was delighted, while my lovesick friend was miserable.

I hope the man from al-Khalil doesn't go on telling jokes. A funny remark generated spontaneously in the course of a conversation, being a sign of wit and quick mindedness, makes me laugh more than jokes that have been learned by heart. Fortunately he stops and doesn't say another word for the rest of the journey.

The car climbs a slight slope and then returns to the level as it regains the paved road.

I think about starting a conversation with the sad young man next to me but quickly drop the idea.

Mahmoud the driver appears relaxed now that we're on the smooth highway. He searches among the buttons on the car's radio, switches it off, and picks up his cell phone.

"Fine. Fine. Thanks."

He reduces speed without explanation.

He looks right and left before turning off the highway, dropping down into a field next to the road, and turning back the way he came.

The comfort of the asphalt has lasted only a few minutes.

He goes another short distance and then explains things to us: "We've just avoided a flying checkpoint. Why the long face, Hajj? 'The hopes of the optimist are rewarded.' 'Every knot finds someone to untie it.'"

"It's all in God's hands, my son," says the Hajj.

"Are you taking us back to Ramallah? My plane leaves tonight and if I miss it I'll lose my scholarship and my whole chance of university," says the young man sitting next to me in a polite voice as though speaking to himself, hoping to hear something reassuring.

The driver replies in a voice that is fatherly, despite their closeness in age. "I've never taken a passenger back where he came from, no matter what. I just need you to help if necessary. That's all I ask of all

9

of you. Don't worry. Smile, Hajj. Lighten up. They want us paralyzed and terrified. They don't realize we've got used to it. And you, my friend—your plane won't go without you. I've never taken a passenger back. Put your faith in God and in me, everyone. Hopefully, everything'll be fine."

A few minutes later he leaves the fields again for an unpaved road.

I'm not familiar with these roads that Mahmoud is taking, and not just because my geographical memory has faded during the years of exile; the sad and now certain truth is that I no longer know the geography of my own land. However, the car is now traveling over open country and there's no sign of paved roads, traffic lights, or human beings as far as the eye can see. It's going across fields and I don't know how this is going to get us to Jericho.

Puddles of water, stones, and wild plants, scattered through a fog that is starting gradually to lift. Everywhere you look, huge olive trees, uprooted and thrown over under the open sky like dishonored corpses. I think: these trees have been murdered, and this plain is their open collective grave. With each olive tree uprooted by the Israeli bulldozers, a family tree of Palestinian peasants falls from the wall. The olive in Palestine is not just agricultural property. It is people's dignity, their news bulletin, the talk of their village guesthouses during evening gatherings, their central bank when profit and loss are reckoned, the star of their dining tables, the companion to every bite they eat. It's the identity card that doesn't need stamps or photos and whose validity doesn't expire with the death of the owner but points to him, preserves his name, and blesses him anew with every grandchild and each season. The olive is the fruit itself (berries that may be any shade of green, any shade of black, or a shiny purplish color; that may be almond-shaped or oblong, oval or spherical) and it is recipes, processes, and tastes (semi-crushed, salted, semi-dried, scored, or stuffed with almonds or carrots or sweet red pepper). Olives are people's social status and what they're good at. The season of their harvest, in the magical autumn, transforms the men, women, and children of the village into bards, singers, and lyric poets whose rhythms turn the tiring work into a picnic and a collective joy. The olive is the pressed oil flowing from the enormous palm-fiber pressing mats, its puzzling color somewhere between shining green and dark gold. Of the virgin oil produced from the first picking they make each other their most eloquent gifts and in the jars set in rows in the courtyards of their houses they store their peace of mind as well as the indispensable basis of their daily meals. If anyone falls ill, the oil is his medicine, and if they rub their aches with it, the pain goes away (or rather it doesn't, but they believe it does). From its waste, they manufacture soap in the courtyards of their houses and distribute it to the groceries—Shak'a Soap, Tuqan Soap, Nabulsi Hasan Shaheen Soap, and others. From the wood produced by the annual pruning, they carve curios, lovely wooden models of mosques and churches, and crosses. With great skill they whittle pictures of the Last Supper, the Manger, and Christ's birth, and statuettes of the Virgin Mary. They fashion arabesque work boxes of various sizes inlaid with mother-of-pearl from the Dead Sea, along with necklaces and rosaries, horses and camel caravans, and carve them to the smoothness, luster, and amazing hardness of ivory. From the crushed olive stones they extract smooth grindings that they use as a fuel for their stoves along with or instead of charcoal, and over whose silent fire they roast chestnuts during the 'forty days' of the bitterest cold, leaving the coffee pot to simmer gently, quietly, over its slow heat while outside the thunder mountains collapse, gather, and then collapse again, preceded by lightning at times hesitant, at times peremptory. Next to these stoves they exchange their sly humor, make fun of their cruel situation, practice their masterful skill at friendly backbiting, and, when the visits of relatives or neighbors bring a boy and a girl together in one house, exchange flirtatious glances that combine daring with shyness. For those who don't like coffee, they bring the blue tea pot, and sage leaves with their intoxicating perfume of the mountains.

These trees have been murdered, I think, and at the same instant, in two different places, stand a peasant with empty hands and a soldier filled with pride; in the same room of night a Palestinian peasant stares at the ceiling and an Israeli soldier celebrates.

The fine rain continues.

The road becomes more rugged.

Our shoulders touch with each jolt.

The veiled lady presses herself more and more tightly against the door of the car; she has placed her bag between her and the young man as an extra layer of insulation, for greater peace of mind.

No one starts a conversation on any topic.

Everyone is worrying about arriving safely, without anyone appearing to be worrying about arriving safely.

This is how it always is: just as the drunken man proves his drunkenness by denying it, so people's denial of their fear proves they are scared.

Suddenly, everything stops.

Now, with the car stuck in the mud, Mahmoud turns off the engine, so that the tires don't dig in deeper and complicate matters further.

We get out to see what's happened.

It seems the situation isn't serious. The problem can be fixed.

"A little push, everyone."

We gather, form a scrum at the back of the car, and push, making several attempts before we succeed in freeing it. I convince myself that I'm playing an effective role in pushing the car even though I depend on the zeal of the others, which seems so clear when compared to the amount of strength that I demonstrate. The old man's keenness and the young woman's determination and enthusiasm amaze me. She is the only one to do her job with the cheerfulness of a child, encouraging us at the same time with loud cries: "Come on, boys! Put your backs into it, boys!"

The old man, happy to have been included among the 'boys,' tells her, "God bless your youth, cousin!"

Given how difficult it is for him, the fat man stands out as the one among us who gives the most of himself, while the countryman who had been sunk in his seat provides conclusive evidence that he is very short indeed. I suppress a smile, as I remember Subhi al-Far, the peasant from Deir Ghassanah who returned from the village threshing floors to give the men in the village guesthouse the good news of a bumper wheat harvest that year and exclaimed with great joy, "The harvest this year is fantastic, God protect it! As tall as me, exactly."

Abu 'Odeh, the guesthouse's best and wittiest talker, said, "God widow your wife, Subhi al-Far! If the wheat's your height, we'll all die of hunger this year!"

Mahmoud drives the car a few meters forward and stops to wait for us. We call to the lady in the veil to catch up; she has stood off to one side during the rescue operation.

The mud sticks to our clothes, our hands, our shoes. Mahmoud fetches a small jerry can of water from the trunk of the car.

"Everyone take turns, now. Please, sister. Please, Hajj. Please, Mister."

One by one, each of us washes his hands as he carefully measures out the water. He offers us a piece of cloth from inside the car with which we try to wipe off the bits of mud that have stuck to our clothes and we use up a box of paper tissues drying our faces.

It's still day but it looks like evening because of the thickness of the fog in the valley. No doubt Mahmoud has 20/20 vision and no doubt his relative quiet helps him to concentrate his eyesight to the utmost. Now he's whispering that he's spotted a concealed Israeli tank and that we have to wait a little to see if it'll go away.

We stop.

After a few minutes he decides the danger is past.

We continue on our way.

I think to myself, a person could cross this valley on foot; horses or mules could find their way through these rocky twists and turns; but how can an old taxi carrying seven passengers and their luggage do so, with the fog and the rain closing in and the Israeli 'Defense' Force in its hideouts behind the trees? I think: this young Palestinian is trying to perform a small miracle without realizing it, is being a hero unaware that he's being a hero. He's only a hired driver but he wants to do the job that earns him his monthly salary perfectly. Right now, he's the leader of this trip and doesn't want to let us down. We are now his nation—an old man and two women (one of whom doesn't cover her hair and face while the other wears a full veil); a man who's short and another who's fat; a university student; and a poet who is amazed by everything he sees and doesn't want to spoil it by talking.

What would you do if you were in his place, I ask myself.

Would I be capable of leading this trip?

I am a writer, that is, I don't 'do' anything. Isn't that pathetic?

Or am I just being too quick to blame myself, as I always am when things go wrong around me?

How often I've wished I'd learned some craft, some manual trade. Isn't it beautiful for a person to be a mechanic, a smith, a farmer, a carpenter, an engineer, a doctor, or even a construction worker with strong muscles who rises with each additional story to a higher rank and at the end looks out over the lazy city from above? He owes no one any favors, for he has raised himself by the sweat of his hands and now sees what the hawk sees, even if he leaves his glory behind and flies away forgotten after the inauguration night. One day my mother caught sight of me. I was twelve and my mother could see me trying to dig the green-onion bed in the vegetable garden with my younger brother Majid. We were breathing hard and she said with a smile as she stood at the top of the steps to the house, "It'll have to be school for you, my boys, that's for sure. You'll die of hunger if you ever have to work with your hands."

Then she came down the short flight of steps, took the hoe from me, and started whacking the vegetable bed while we watched. I don't know how Majid felt but I was jealous and embarrassed. When I was a child I thought my muscles were weak because I was thin. I heard someone say that potatoes 'build you up' so I went overboard on potatoes in all forms in the hope that my muscles would harden. Whenever my mother asked the question she asked every morning as we made for the front door on our way to school—"What shall I cook for you today?"—I'd turn my head and beat my brothers to it by saying, "Potato casserole."

She took me seriously once or twice. Then she started making fun of me and I became an easy target for my brothers' jokes. When I published my first collection of poems, I was pleased with how thin I was. In moments of stupidity (which fortunately didn't last very long), I'd wonder at the 'blooming good health' of Pablo Neruda, because he looked like a bank director—as though a poet had to look wasted, half dead, and pale, like someone who's fallen into a chasm or just been pulled out of one!

Now we're faced with a real chasm.

The driver stops the engine.

"Get out, everyone. We'll have a look and see what we can do."

We get out.

And we see.

We are on the edge of a cutting across the road that the rains have transformed into a huge, impromptu, mud-filled trench that the car will not be able to cross unless a Greek god from the heavens of myth, capable of changing fates, appears and gets us out of this earthly fix.

Our driver has improvised our present route through this gray valley. He has remained in control, more or less, no matter how much it has twisted and turned and narrowed, so long as it has been uninterrupted, but now it's cut; it isn't a road any more. And this long, deep trench could swallow dozens of cars.

The man from al-Khalil says, "It must be my fault. I'm unlucky by nature. I've been that way all my life. If there are a thousand tins of milk at the supermarket, I'll pick the one that's gone bad."

I tell him about Abu Wajih, who was a ploughman in our village. Once a friend of his found him exhausted from ploughing a huge olive field and told him, "Your work will soon be done, Abu Wajih, and then you can rest."

Abu Wajih answered, "I swear to God, if the Resurrection comes and I go to paradise, I'll find no rest. If there's land to be ploughed in paradise, the Almighty will say, 'Arise, Abu Wajih, and plough it.' You think He's going to ask Abdel Halim Hafez?"

Mahmoud doesn't look worried. In fact, he looks as confident and calm as if the Greek gods were his first cousins.

In just a few minutes, a giant yellow crane appears from among the trees on the other side of the trench, glistening under the drizzle. In it are two thin, poorly dressed youths, one of whom gestures to Mahmoud to prepare for the rescue.

Later, years after this incident, I will cross a similar trench at the Surda checkpoint on foot in the company of a group of foreign writers who are our guests and whose program includes a visit to Birzeit University. Our cars leave Ramallah in convoy and halt at the Surda checkpoint, halfway to the university. The Israeli army has previously destroyed the mountain road by making a kind of trench in it about 500 meters long that can be crossed only on foot, and with difficulty at that. On a hilltop next to the road stands a large house belonging to a Palestinian family that the army has occupied after throwing out the residents and has converted into both a military post monitoring everything that moves and an operations room where the decision to close the road can be taken at any time. The entire front of the building is covered with green camouflage material pierced with holes and through these can be seen the barrels of machine guns pointed at the people going through the checkpoint. The cars that have brought us from Ramallah stop and we get out to cross the trench on foot. I keep up my conversation about theater with Wole Soyinka and we try to avoid stumbling. Around us the others are continuing their discussions on literature and politics, their bodies approaching and separating according to the unevenness of the dug-out area. Saramago, Goytisolo, Breytenbach, Consolo, Bei Dao, and Mahmoud Darwish move forward inside the trench with the caution of the elderly, returning the greetings of the students, teachers, and traveling salesmen who walk beside them, for this rough trench is the only road for those traveling between Ramallah and the villages of the north. It's been this way for a whole year. Wole Soyinka pulls me to one side to make way for a young man carrying an aged peasant woman on his back. He proceeds with extreme caution while she keeps repeating, "God damn them in this world and the next!" and readjusting her headscarf, gripping its ends between her teeth so that it doesn't slip off her white hair completely. Another old woman, a foreigner, is walking next to a donkey in whose panniers are two suitcases from each of which dangles a Delsey tag, specifying the luxury brand. The Delsey factory can never have imagined that donkeys would carry their suitcases here. A few meters further on we make way for another donkey, ridden by a pregnant woman and led by a boy of seven or a little more. Clearly, he makes his living hiring the donkey out at the checkpoint. He looks around, bemused at finding foreign faces in this corner of the world. Saramago, contemplating the scene and turning to the hills, the houses of the Palestinian villagers, and the guns of the Israeli army pointed at us from a distance, says to Leila Shahid, our ambassador to France, in his deep, extremely dignified, voice, "Leila, this reminds me of a concentration camp. The people here are living in a concentration camp. It's a true concentration camp. That's what I think."

After crossing the trench, we will climb up to the highway and get into different cars, sent by the Birzeit administration to wait for us on the other side so that we can finish our journey to the university.

This morning, however, things are quite different.

We are now in front of a trench similar to the one at Surda but we're in a taxi carrying large, medium, and small suitcases on its roof and with seven passengers inside, and it is this car and no other that has to get us to the other side. It is this car and no other that has to take us to Jericho; there is no alternative in this remote stretch of country. There is no way back and there are no taxis waiting on the other side of this fissure in the earth.

It occurs to Mahmoud that he ought to secure the suitcases with rope to prevent all or some of them from falling off during the rescue operation. He fetches a long rope, ties one end to the luggage rack, throws it over to the other side, tugs on it, and then repeats the procedure, helped by the sad young man, who comes quickly to his assistance. He doesn't stop tying till he's completely satisfied. He orders us to return to our seats inside the car so that the two rescuers can start their work. We sit and wait.

Mahmoud issues his instructions: "Fasten your seat belts. Don't panic. We're going for a ride on the swings!"

He laughs, to encourage us and himself.

He takes his place behind the wheel, first making sure that the doors are properly closed.

A moment of total silence envelops us all. A moment as silent as a candle burning. A moment as silent as a letter being passed under a door.

Then the rumbling begins.

Dumbstruck, I watch what's happening.

The huge long arm of the crane rises gradually into space until it reaches what its drivers judge to be the correct height. Its metal joints rub and chitter against one another and from time to time it groans as they lower the arm slowly toward us, tilting it a little to the left, then a little to the right, and finally, with extreme care, bringing it down till it is almost touching the car. Next, it takes the car in the grip of its terrible iron fingers, which wrap themselves around its body like the fingers of a hand around a pomegranate, and with careful slowness lifts it, and us, into the air. We are now between earth and sky.

The suspended bubble of air in which we seven are swinging is now our place of exile from this earth. It is our disabled will and our attempt, in a mixture of courage and fear, to impose our will through wit and cunning. This bubble of air is the unyielding Occupation itself. It is the rootless roaming of the Palestinians through the air of others' countries. In the world's air we seek refuge from our earth. We sink into the upper spaces. We sink upward. God rest the soul of Salvador Dali, who (being dead) will never be able to picture this scene. This absurd bubble of air is Mahmoud's way of letting no obstacle defeat him and force him to take us back in failure. Now the wish of those who, like us at this moment, have risen high, is to become low. I absolve my grandmother from any blame; she would call down blessings on me, boy and young man, and say, "Go, Mourid, son of Sakina my daughter, may God elevate your rank!" or "God raise high your standing among men!" The only high place I've achieved among men, Grandmother, and the only high rank I've risen to in my country is thanks to this deaf metal monster. Did you pray to the heavens so often for my 'elevation' that they decided to answer your prayers like this and mock us both? I want my high standing to be brought low, Grandmother. I want to descend from this regal elevation and touch the mud and dust once more so that I can be an ordinary traveler again. The Occupation is these moments of loneliness between man's earth and the sky.

We stare downward out of the windows of the car. Yes, downward! Our dream now, Grandmother, is at the level of our feet. We stare at the abyss and the abyss stares at us. The screeching of the crane and the groaning of its metal joints rise and fall as we move away from the edge behind us and closer to the hoped-for edge on the other side.

The crane backs up a little.

Its flying arm, carrying us through the fog of the valley, tries to transfer us, with care, from one edge to another. The crane backs up again and stops.

We arrive.

The metal fingers move away from the body of the car, leaving it to make gentle contact with the earth.

The mechanical swing puts us safely down.

We all get out and the two Greek gods join us.

Everyone hugs everyone else (except for the veiled lady, who stands to one side, away from our crowding emotions). We find ourselves clapping as we stand there, as though celebrating an historic victory.

"Thanks, everyone. Good work."

Mahmoud passes out coffee cups. Coffee and its timing, again. It's not quite as hot but it's still good, having now acquired the taste of reward for a job well done. I savor two cigarettes, lighting the second from the first and sharing with Mahmoud, the man from al-Khalil, and our two rescuers the pleasure of sheltering our cigarettes from the rain.

The old man moves away from us without explanation, disappears behind a nearby tree for a few minutes, and then returns, fastening the buckle of his leather belt and apologizing with obvious embarrassment for holding us up.

"Goddamn diabetes. Sorry everyone, I've held you up."

The two mysterious rescuers wish us a successful end to our journey. They drive the crane back to its hiding place behind the trees, perhaps to wait for another rescue mission or to get ready to make a speedy return to their village before the soldiers discover what they're up to.

The engine is turned on again.

The car moves forward along the valley.

After a period of bucking and rocking, the silk of asphalt takes us by surprise. We look at one another in relief and joy, as though it were a dream fulfilled, as though we'd scored a victory over someone.

Peoples under occupation may be among those most given to festivity and most ready to celebrate. This, of course, is directly opposed to the picture of grossness and cruelty that the enemy and the stereotype-obsessed media draw of them. Under occupation, you experience true pleasure just because you've managed to get hold of a cylinder of butane gas, a pile of loaves of bread, a pass, or a seat on the bus. You feel joy at finding blood pressure pills at the chemist's, at the arrival of the ambulance before some sick person close to you dies. You get pleasure from reaching home safely and finding that the electricity has been turned back on. You feel ecstasy at being able to walk on the beach. You dance for joy at the most trivial victory in anything, even a card game. In its most subtle form, this human fragility may take on legendary proportions, when your endless patience becomes in and of itself soft pillows protecting you from nightmares.

I look at the paved road surface and a verse leaps into my mind from a poem by Muhammad Mahdi al-Jawahiri, who lived through both dictatorship and occupation in his native Iraq:

Fortunate Tigris, how have our ambitions shrunk—
Yet even the least ambitious of our aspirations is in doubt.

Well said, poet!

Hasn't our most exalted aspiration on this blessed morning been to reach the asphalt, to reach, what, in the end, is no more than tar?

Did it ever occur to you, Mr. Jawahiri, that tar could be an aspiration? Did it ever occur to you that a road paved with tar could become the dream of a nation?

You have to imagine it, Mr. Jawahiri!

You really ought to imagine it.

Otherwise, what would be the meaning of the Occupation?

We enjoy a few smooth kilometers on the road. We achieve our ambition and in the distance the outskirts of Jericho appear.

Later, friends and relations used to moving between Palestine and Jordan via the bridge will explain that what happened to me on my strange journey is an everyday experience, especially the business with the crane that moves stranded cars. The Israelis know that on days when there are closures we take side roads to avoid their checkpoints, so they've taken to cutting them using dynamite and bulldozers to create chasms, trenches, and dikes that cars can't cross. And what has happened? The villagers and nearby shepherds have come up with this method of helping others and themselves too. They hire this giant winch with a grab from a builder's yard and take a hundred shekels for each car they rescue. Why not? It's their labor. What matters is that for every obstacle the Occupation sets, Palestinian desperation finds a solution.

I hear Mahmoud's voice.

"From here to Jericho there's no army, no checkpoints, no cranes, and no swings in the air. Praise God for a safe arrival, everyone!"

Laughing, the fat man says, "And you got me onto the swings at my age, boys! I'd never been on one before. I used to get dizzy just looking at the Ferris wheel and wonder how the little kids could ride it. We've become a spectacle, I swear. God bring it all down on their heads!"

I want to tell him the story of how once, in a violent storm, Tamim and his friend Zeid got stuck at the top of the Ferris wheel at the kids' amusement park in Budapest and were rescued, but decide it wouldn't be appropriate in our present situation. That was the second reason; the first was that I've got used to not talking if I'm with people I don't know in a car or a bus or line. You never know which way a conversation with strange traveling companions may turn. A question you ask, or your answer to a question, may be embarrassing or dangerous or stir up a painful memory, or so I convinced myself some time ago. Also, under Occupation, you may find yourself learning things you're not supposed to, and who knows what difficulties your tongue may get you into? You may indicate your admiration for the resistance fighters and fugitives in the mountains who are wanted by Israel and tell the story of one of them whom you know because he's a relation, friend, or neighbor, and the person you're talking to may be an Israeli agent, of whom there are thousands, unfortunately. Israel has made it a condition (accepted by our very clever negotiators) that the Palestinian leadership does not have the right to punish, pursue, or even try them. They move among us, some of them known to all. You may find yourself at a ceremony of mourning for a martyr while, because of rural family bonds, an agent—the martyr's cousin, for example, or his in-law—receives condolences for his relative the 'hero,' and the agent's mourning for the deceased may be genuine too. This has actually occurred in Deir Ghassanah, just as it has in other villages, and it will continue to. There are plenty of other risks also—such as spoiling the atmosphere with an unfunny joke, as the man from al-Khalil had done. Nevertheless, all these possibilities taken together neither explain nor justify my position, which in fact isn't justifiable. What's certain, though, is that my aversion to talking makes me seem aloof. Some may accuse me of being stuck-up—which is unbecoming for someone with a political cause—and

I cannot defend this fault and I won't justify it. Man's biggest fault is to deny his faults and defend them to the death. It's true too that my aloofness results in my losing the beautiful friendships that traveling with others might lead to under ordinary circumstances. The Occupation, however, permits no ordinary circumstances. The Occupation distorts the distances between humans as much as those between places. I wonder about this idea, which has just occurred to me and which I shall give more thought to soon.

When one is lifted off the ground, a certain loneliness and sense of isolation combine with the unexpected loftiness. This is true whatever the vehicle, be it a swing or an elevator or an airplane. This leads to me think about Mahmoud's coming loneliness and my worries about him.

A question now comes into my head that will preoccupy me for many years: how will Mahmoud get back alone to Ramallah under these extraordinary circumstances?

Doesn't he give any thought to the dangers of the ruined, muddy roads that await him as he returns to his family after a day's work that was supposed to be routine but was anything but routine?

Will he go back today?

Will he spend the night in Jericho and wait till the morning?

And what if the closure lasts for days?

I admire his poise and ability. Indeed, his conduct, liveliness, youth, and confidence now seduce me into a burst of optimism that sees the Palestinians as the stronger side in this long conflict with the Occupation. All I need is an inspired idea on how to thank this boy without insulting what he did with empty, worn-out words.

The moment he hugs me I decide that the best I have to offer is silence.

I throw out the fleeting idea of offering the young man extra money in less than a second.

I consider a strange paradox. One may easily get into a quarrel with an opponent and slip without thinking into uttering the most vulgar words, which you will later regret—but find it difficult to choose a pleasant word with which to praise a friend. Some forms of gratitude demean the gift, sometimes, and that's what I'm afraid of in this case.

I'm jealous of his determination and his abilities and I admire him to the point of feeling proud of him, but I can't tell him that because the very word has something of the patronizing or the paternalistic or the classist about it that cancels our equality as humans. How am I supposed to convey this 'pride' to him? With a tip?

I'm worried about him.

I think of telling him, "Take care of yourself," but don't.

That tender and loving phrase is the most beautiful thing one can hear from a person who's important to you when you part. My mother used to say it every time I left the house, or traveled for a job or other purpose. "Take care of yourself."

"How am I to take care of myself, Mother?"

If an Arab ruler wishes to arrest me, he will without doubt arrest me.

If a policeman wants to kick me in the stomach and liver, he will without doubt kick me.

If an esteemed 'sovereign' Arab sister-state wishes to exercise its 'sovereignty' against my thin body or my innocuous words in order to kick me out with its imported shoes, it will kick me out.

I want to tell him "God be with you" and immediately smile at an unforgettable anecdote about God's lack of support for the Palestinians. This was explained on the one hand by the repeated assertion of Sheikh Qaysar, muezzin of the mosque of Deir Ghassanah, that God wasn't standing by us because we'd "abandoned His religion." On the other was the comment of Hajja Umm Nabil, nearly maddened by the Arab defeat of 1967 and Israel's six-day (really six-hour) victory over

Egypt, Syria, and Jordan. Hajja Umm Nabil raised her arms in the face of a reporter who didn't know her language and yelled at the top of her voice, "Performing our prayers didn't help us and keeping the fasts didn't get us in with Him either, sonny. It turns out the Almighty wears a kipa and shorts. If He curled his side-locks, He'd be perfect." Sensing that anger had drawn her into saying something rather odd that didn't go with her instinctive piety, she then muttered to herself, "I seek God's forgiveness! It's enough to make heathens of us."

I say nothing to Mahmoud. To myself I say, "I'll write him. I'll write the driver Mahmoud. And I'll put down exactly what he did and how he did it. I'll write him. It's my duty. I'm a writer and that's my job. He did his job and one day I'll do mine too." And here I am doing it.

We reach the Jericho resthouse.

We get our bags down and each of us pays Mahmoud the fare plus his share of the cost of hiring the divinely blessed crane.

The bus for the bridge is standing waiting for passengers. We put our bags into the compartments allocated for them under the bus.

We say goodbye to Mahmoud.

He shakes our hands and wishes us a good journey to Amman.

I stand in a disorganized line where everyone is pushing, waiting to get my papers stamped.

In the long line next to mine, I see the veiled lady raise her veil hesitantly from her face. The Israeli policewoman tells her to remove it completely, which she does. Clearly the policewoman wants the security cameras or the officer seated behind tinted glass in the raised booth to identify the traveler's face properly.

The people in the line surge about trying to get ahead of each other, those at the front of the line protesting at the others who are bothering them. The voice of a short, bald man in the line is heard: "Keep to the line, please. Have some manners. Let's get on our way."

He might as well have been talking to the deaf.

The Israeli officer notices the disturbance. He stands up and yells at everyone to form a single line.

They do so immediately.

Between the Israeli police post on the bridge and the Jordanian police post, we have to change buses. The first bus delivers us to a dusty lot around which our suitcases are dropped in scattered piles so roughly that bits of them generally get damaged or their contents are strewn everywhere. In all cases, it ensures that they get dirty, especially on rainy days. Then we have to get out, pushing and shoving like a repulsive human herd whose individual members are so selfish that the elderly, the slow-moving, and the polite are ignored among the struggles of each passenger to find his bag in the middle of the chaotic pile into which it has been thrown and then put it with his own hands onto the new bus that will travel the short distance to the Jordanian police station.

Someone whom I take from his accent to be from Nablus shouts, "Have you made your ablutions, Muhammad?"

"Sure, Dad. I performed the ablutions, praise be to God."

"Okay, let's get the afternoon prayer in quickly then."

"Did you hear the call to prayer, Dad?"

"Damn it, you're a fool. Who's going to give the call to prayer here? You're wearing a watch the size of a wall clock and it's prayer time."

Amid the scattered suitcases, the man from Nablus and his son stand up to perform the prayer and a number of male passengers join them, so the rest of us have to wait until they're done. It's a new phenomenon in society, this public display of Islam.

We sit in the new bus waiting for them and then leave for the Jordanian police post. We arrive. A Jordanian policeman gets in, collects the IDs and passports from all the passengers, and leaves, after ordering the driver to keep the doors closed until he is given permission to open them by the officials on the other side.

In this spot in summer, temperature and humidity reach their highest levels in the world, sometimes rising to 50 degrees Celsius, even though the meteorological authorities, for reasons I don't understand, record them as being only in the upper forties. It's winter now and waiting does no harm, but having to wait again each time is annoying. During this wait too I retreat into my shell.

I'm alone with sounds and sights, with my private question marks and exclamation marks.

It's as though a huge deserted warehouse had opened its doors to me or I'd become my own museum and its only visitor after the guards have gone home to sleep and locked me in.

I find fault with my acts, or the fewness of them, or the total lack of them, or their total ineffectiveness. I confront my faults like a courageous hero of the stage or make up hypocritical excuses for myself like any coward.

I become a severe judge who refuses to accept the arguments of the self, lovers, or relatives, and, in the same instant, I become the conniving, bribable judge who flees difficulties in favor of peace of mind.

I open my small eyes to the 'intellectual's diseases' that have taken root in my body.

I say to myself, I'm just a poet. Why should I have to wait at all the different types of border?

Why can't I put up with what the fat grandmothers, the young ploughmen with their handsome bronze faces, and the children, who have got used to the Occupation, put up with—so much so that they have, to everyone's surprise, forced it into a tight spot?

I hear a voice inside me proclaiming its revulsion at the lack of backbone of some poets and writers and their constant whining. I feel that in the end I'm a bad person when compared to these people who make so many sacrifices without complaining.

I tell myself no writer deserves glory so long as his people are in torment, even if he's the person best able to give expression to that suffering. People may honor him because they value his talent or his role but he will be mistaken if he thinks that's the end of the matter.

I think, I wish I were a train. A train doesn't wait. Nor does a farmer. All a farmer waits for is the rainy season, which is easier than waiting for this bus to move before I go out of my mind.

I want to get to the house.

I want to sleep.

The Jordanian policeman allows us to get off the bus. We proceed to the passport barrier, then to our bags, and then to the street.

In a little while the sun will start to set. I'll be in our house in al-Shmaysani before my mother goes to sleep.

Once I've crossed the bridge and entered Jordanian territory, peace enters my soul. I start to feel that things are at least normal again. I become a tranquil traveler. I can enjoy the sight of the trees running alongside the car and contemplate the banana plantations, the oleander flowers, and the roads that have no checkpoints, barriers, or watch-towers. To one leaving Occupied Palestine, Jordan seems like a truly blessed place. No being stopped, no settlements, and no tanks. Here distances always measure the same. You know how many minutes you need to get from one place to another. I take a car to Amman because I want to be on my own. I want to go over this whole journey in my mind from the beginning. I have half an hour to go before I arrive. I put my Jordanian SIM card in my cell phone and call Radwa in Cairo.

"I'm finally on my way to al-Shmaysani."

Then I call my mother in Amman.

"What's for dinner, Mother?"

Next morning, the dead and wounded lie scattered in their hundreds.

Television screens are colored red, almost shattered by the shells from the tanks, which hammer at life without let-up. The long embroidered dresses of the mothers bend over the faces of the dead and their arms shake the bodies in their shrouds in the hope of reviving life, if only to bid it farewell. Their hands call before their lips can to those who will never hear a mother's or a sister's or a grandmother's voice again until the end of time.

All news bulletins start with the news of the Israeli army's invasion of Ramallah.

2

Father and Son

The moment has come. Radwa says goodbye to us at Cairo Airport. She hugs Tamim. She hugs me.

The three of us hug one another, holding as still as the marble base of a clamorous fountain whose water tries to touch the sky before being reclaimed by the earth with the violence of gravity.

We pause for a moment.

As though none of us wants to leave the place.

"Let me know how things are going, blow by blow."

"Don't worry. Tamim will enter, get the ID very quickly, God willing, and return to you and his university safe and sound."

"Bye. Lots of greetings from me to Mama Umm Mounif."

"We'll call you as soon as we get to Amman."

Once again we start the journey from Cairo to Amman and from there to the bridge.

Since my first crossing in 1996, after thirty years of exile, I have crossed many times, sometimes with ease and sometimes with difficulty. I've seen Israeli soldiers whose seriousness, which can rise to the level of scowls of superiority, never leaves them and others who practice their job with professionalism, as though they were customs inspectors and nothing more. In the eyes of some, I've seen a certain confusion and, very occasionally, I've seen one who smiles or shows some desire to be of help. There is no homogeneity to their features—Ethiopian, Brooklynite, Slavic, Yemeni. The common factor is that they're all armed. Some are newly conscripted adolescents, male and female, and some of these seem bewildered by their daily contact with hundreds of the Arab 'enemy.' In all cases, though, the rifles are ready for use at any moment. Taken together, they constitute a nightmare for every Palestinian who crosses the bridge. It's difficult to trust the smile of a person carrying weapons here.

Our problem with the Jew, here in this 'Jewish State' as they insist on calling it, is that all three or four generations of Palestinians have seen of him is his helmet. They've seen the Jew only in khaki, with his finger on the rifle's trigger. They've seen him only as a sniper at a window, an officer in a tank, a conscript at a checkpoint, a guard clacking his metal heels past the doors to prison cells or along the long corridors that separate them, or a heavy hand in the interrogation rooms, where Israeli law allows the use of what they call 'moderate physical force' (!) to extract confessions. Many western journalists who maintain a studied and malign blindness to the Occupation have asked me whether the Palestinian people are really ready to coexist with the Jews and I reply that we coexisted with them for hundreds of years in Palestine, the Arab countries, and Andalusia, and that it is Europe, which reproves us and holds us to account, that couldn't coexist with them and sent millions of them mercilessly to the Holocaust. What is asked of us today, however, and has been ever since their military occupation of our land, is to coexist with their tanks in our bedrooms! Show me one person in this world, I say to them, who can live with a tank in his bedroom.

The cliché has it that bridges are symbols of communication, connection, and coexistence. This bridge is a symbol of discrimination, distance, disunion, and the historic distinction between the frightener and the frightened, though sometimes it is hard to be sure who fears the other more. Have the meanings of 'bridge' found in the dictionary been so completely distorted that they are no longer useful for describing this bridge? The Israeli obsession with security makes this bridge a great gap, a chasm with teeth. Everything in Israel is determined by its obsession with security. It is a nation that sees itself as forever victorious, forever frightened, and forever in the right. It has been victorious, and frightened, for sixty years. Always, whether fighting or negotiating, it enjoys the support of the only superpower in today's world, as well as of all the European states. It also enjoys the secret collusion of twenty debased Arab regimes. It is a state that possesses more than two hundred nuclear warheads, has erected more than six hundred barriers and checkpoints, has built around us a wall 780 kilometers long, detains more than eleven thousand prisoners, controls all borders and crossing points leading to our country by land, sea, and air, and frames its laws with reference to a permanent philosophy that its victories do not change, a philosophy whose core is this mighty state's fear . . . of us.

Here is a truly frightening state. The Israeli military pilot climbs the skies over any Palestinian city and flies his intimidating F-16 or Apache with as much peace of mind as if he were piloting a Swissair or an Air France plane, and releases his cluster, fragmentation, and phosphorus bombs and aims his 'smart' rockets at any target he wishes. The city is fair game, an easy target spread out beneath him. The Palestinians do not have anti-aircraft weapons. The pilot has become a deadly sky and we a murdered earth. The pilot returns safe to his wife or girl friend in Tel Aviv and talks to her of his 'victory' over the Palestinians! Despite this, Israel behaves like a state that is truly terrified and fills the world with cries that its existence is threatened. Could Orwell have imagined a more flagrant abuse of language than this?

I think this over and say to myself that it is our 'moderate' leaders, who fear victory and make no preparations for it, who give Israel the impression that it will never know anything but victory while we will never know anything but defeat. Those whom the West describes as 'moderate Arabs' are the type of politicians who prefer to spend their lives waiting for a smile from the Israeli Occupation's tank. They are out of luck because the tank never smiles. The tank, you wise and clever realists, doesn't know how to smile.

Some years later, I will enter Ramallah in an ambulance though neither injured nor suffering a medical emergency. On the bridge and at the numerous checkpoints, I will see numerous faces, situations, oddities, and tragedies. This time, though, my feelings are more complex and mixed. My anxiety is as painful as if I were being beaten over and over without a chance to hit back. 'Painful' is the right word. Has anxiety ever made you feel pain? The anxiety is all the more painful because I have to conceal it, have to pretend the opposite and appear supremely confident and at ease, for now, this specific time, I shall be crossing the bridge with Tamim.

This is his day.

A day he and we—Radwa and I—have been waiting for since I applied for an entry permit for him two years ago. Now his entry permit is in my pocket. I would have liked us to enter some time in summer so that he wouldn't be forced to leave his studies at the university, where he's in his fourth, crucial, graduation year, but it's beyond our control. It's always beyond our control. Otherwise, what would be the meaning of the Occupation?

Radwa showed no sign of the agitation that ought to accompany her farewell to her only child before a journey such as this. Or did she,

I wonder, conceal her agitation precisely because he was setting off to repossess the personal, tangible Palestine that she had raised him to be aware belonged to him, as he to it, with all that that implies?

This wasn't what moved me when she hugged him with exceptional warmth at Cairo Airport. What moved me was her silent care not to appear the party 'sacrificing' its peace of mind for the sake of a step before which inconvenience must seem trivial and for which difficulties must be borne.

On the plane heading for Amman I think about Radwa.

I read my first poems to her on the steps of the Cairo University library when we were not yet twenty. We took part together in literary gatherings at the Faculty without it occurring to us that a personal interest had developed, or was developing, between us. We were students and limited our conversation to 'professional' matters such as our studies and never went beyond these into any intimate topic. She would tell me, "You will become a poet," and I would reply, "And what if I fail at that?" I'd tell her, "You will become a great novelist" and she'd give the same answer and we'd laugh. This 'fraternal' language and collegial spirit continued between us until the four years of study were over and I went to work in Kuwait. I used to write regular letters about my new life in Kuwait to her and to Amina Sabri and Amira Fahmi, our best friends throughout our studies, with whom we'd made something like a small family. I realized, however, that my letters to Radwa contained nothing of my news or the events of my life and concerned themselves only with my unspoken feelings about that life.

When I saw her on my first visit to Cairo during the summer holidays, we found ourselves talking like a mother and a father, and sometimes like a grandmother and a grandfather. We talked like a family of two that had been together for ages.

It was out of the question to talk about 'steps' we ought to be taking.

It was as though we'd walked all the steps already and got to here.

Talking of our future relationship had become a part of our past relationship, whose precise moment of beginning we never tried to establish. We never engaged in flirting or courtship or questions or arrangements or promises. When I left Cairo and returned to resume my work in Kuwait, I found that I was writing to her as a husband and she was writing to me as a wife.

I often questioned the wisdom of this marriage when I had no land to bear me and no clear plan for our geographical, economic, or social future. Her family naturally stood against it and they were right not to allow their only daughter to marry a non-Egyptian youth whose future was tied to that of the Palestinian issue, which nations and generations had failed to resolve. I didn't blame them for an instant. But she too never thought for one instant of abandoning her decision. This is how I learned courage and clarity of will, from a girl two years younger than I who knew what she wanted and went after it with her eyes open— consciously, calmly, passionately.

Tamim thinks I'm taking a short nap but I hear the flight attendant inviting the passengers to fasten their seat belts in preparation for the descent to Amman Airport.

We spend three days with my mother in Amman. She couldn't let us leave before she'd cooked Tamim his favorite dishes, such as musakhan and chicken with thyme, and listened to him playing the oud and singing her his satirical songs in Egyptian dialect poking fun at his teachers at his secondary school in Cairo. And I couldn't leave her before I'd talked to her about everything that was on my mind and we'd caught up and told one another all about what had and hadn't happened since our last meeting.

This time my friend Damin takes us in his car to the bridge at eight a.m. The time passes without our noticing because he never stops making us laugh with his constantly updated store of jokes and stories.

We present our papers. The Jordanian officer stamps them without delay. We get into a car after paying eighty dollars to the facilitating company and set off immediately instead of waiting for the bus, which doesn't move until it has filled its forty-plus seats—a process that takes an hour at the least. I will do anything in my power to save time. I've told myself that the Israelis can delay us as long as they like when we get to the Israeli side, that's not under my control, but I don't want us to wait on both sides of the border; one is enough.

I want Tamim to enter Palestine before sunset so that he can see it in daylight and I don't want any surprises.

His papers are all in order now. His entry permit is still fresh, with all the seals, stamps, and signatures in Hebrew. Yes, in Hebrew, or else what would be the meaning of the Occupation?

After all the peace agreements, the establishment of the Palestinian National Authority, the propagation, with Israel's consent, of Palestinian flags in its sky and offices, and the talk everywhere of Palestinian independence, no one, whatever his nationality and whatever his origin, can pass through any crossing point into or out of Palestine, by land, sea, or air, without an Israeli entry permit, Israeli stamps, an Israeli security search, and the checking of his or her name against an Israeli blacklist. Interrogation, being sent back to where one came from, arrest and imprisonment in an Israeli jail are all real possibilities. Neither the president of the Authority nor its ministers, officers, judges, security forces, or the members of its 'parliament' are exempt. If the database in the Israeli computer at the crossing point or barrier doesn't like you, no permits, stamps, or visas from before will help you.

Later, Israel will arrest eight Palestinian ministers and twenty-eight elected members of the Palestinian Legislative Council, including 'Aziz al-Duweik, the council's speaker, just because they are members of Hamas. Israel's response to condemnations of this crime is a single sentence, one that has been reused dozens of times, after each abrogation of international law and norms: "No one has immunity here."

Right. No one has immunity here.

Israel is committed to nothing to which Israel does not see fit to commit itself—another bitter fruit of the stupid negotiation with Israel in Oslo to which we sent negotiators whose sole talent lay in being talentless. Their ignorance wasn't the problem, though. The problem was that what took place between them and the Israeli delegation wasn't so much a negotiation as a series of approvals of proposals presented by a team of Israel's shrewdest politicians and lawyers with highly specialized skills in everything needed to make us fall into their visible and invisible traps. On my first visit to Ramallah I said, speaking of our people's attitude to the accords, that they were waiting for the fulfilment of their leaders' promises. Nothing has been fulfilled. There is a huge explosion coming—I don't know where and I don't know when, but the explosion, or explosions, are coming for sure.

At the last Jordanian police post, the officer makes us get out of the car so that he can check our papers and oversee our boarding of the first bus. This bus is unavoidable because entry by car is forbidden to everyone except senior officials of the Palestinian Authority.

I notice someone trying to get an elderly lady out of her wheelchair and onto the bus. This is extremely difficult given her great weight and the high steps to the door of the bus, which is not equipped with a ramp for people with special needs. The paleness of her face makes it clear that she's returning from medical treatment, accompanied by a young man, who welcomes our help in getting her onto the bus and pays no attention to a rude traveler behind us who's annoyed at having to wait.

The bus is full now and the engine is running, but it's waiting for Israeli permission to cross the bridge. In summer, the buses line up in large numbers and wait for the signal, bus by bus. It's just bad luck if you're in one of the ones at the back.

We are on the threshold of Palestine.

We are at the lowest point below sea-level on the planet. Sweat oozes with sticky insistence. Clothes stick annoyingly to bodies. The air here is fried. Daytime in this black hole is a collective curse on all those like us who have to wait, as though the entrance to Palestine were through Hell. There is no way to get there without passing through this harsh spot, lashed by this air and this nature that shows mercy to none.

I tell myself, some homelands are like that: getting into them is hard, getting out of them is hard, and staying in them is hard. And this is the only homeland you have.

The traveler to Palestine does not *cross* its threshold in order to enter, he *dwells* at that threshold for a period that is not determined by him and waits for the instructions of the masters of the house, who determine everything.

I look at the passengers.

My gaze falls on Mr. Namiq al-Tijani and I feel an evil premonition. I do not like to see this Namiq.

The sight of him reminds me of mollusks and mucosities, especially if he smiles or laughs, when his broad gums show and set my nerves on edge.

I say to Tamim in a low voice, "Do you see that person?"

"What about him?"

"He's a very strange creature. Try to observe him. He's the type I can't stand. He's the most representative 'illustrative example' of the generation that is being raised by the Palestinian Authority and I come across him wherever I go. He's a person of symbolic dimensions!"

Tamim doesn't appear interested in my talk of Namiq and is not curious to find out more. He just says, "Forget about him."

I follow his advice and ignore "the Namiq," looking at the other passengers. Palestinian mothers and grandmothers. Peasants with sunny faces and shaven chins, their cheeks bringing to mind the gleam of new swords. Sick people, old people, young people from university, children, merchants, contractors, civil servants from the Authority, expatriates. They prefer not to talk to people they don't know, to avoid problems and in deference to the sense of wariness that haunts people who feel that they're under observation by an obscure power at both ends of the bridge.

I ask myself what has happened to these exhausted, slowly moving grandmothers over the years since my youthful memories of them, when they would walk ten kilometers on foot to reach the springs outside their villages and return carrying their water jugs on their heads, their backs straight. At harvest season, they would pick the olives with their men-folk, quarreling to keep their places in front of the oil press, and receive the guests who came by for a chat in the evening in the courtyards of their houses, where the lemons, mandarins, and pots of basil reflected brilliantly off the windows. That's how I remember my grandmother Umm 'Ata and all the other grandmothers of Deir Ghassanah. I think about the women passengers on the bus, sketching pasts and futures for them as I fancy. Which of them, I wonder, is grandmother to a prisoner or a martyr or a fugitive in the mountains and caves? Which of them is a widow waiting in vain month after month for the National Authority to pay her the support money for her son who is imprisoned in the Ofer, Negev, Nafha, or Ashkelon prisons? Or for the pension for her husband, who sleeps beneath the earth while the radio stations dedicate patriotic songs to his memory and the bearers of the keys to the treasury forget him? What makes her face the misery and annoyances of the bridge and travel to Amman and al-Zarqa and Irbid, to struggle with her baskets and suitcases, with the mistreatment and the vexation of waiting? Is it to meet her second son, who wasn't killed and wasn't arrested, who is coming from his job in the Gulf or from his university in Damascus or London or Canada or the U.S. and who cannot enter Palestine, so that she has to travel in order to see him for one or two days? The Palestinian woman, like any other woman in this world, works, gets things done and brings about change, and I don't know where all these duties of hers come from or how they have piled up on top of her or how she carries them out so well. With death, imprisonment, or exile taking off so many of their sons and male relatives, it is these women who fill the markets, the demonstrations, the workshops making embroidery, olive-wood carvings, arabesque work, mother-of-pearl, and necklaces, and who quarrel with the headmaster about their grandchildren's schoolwork, and it is they who listen to Nawal El Saadawi explaining her implacable feminist revolution on the television without understanding a word she says. I look at them and think of my mother in Amman beseeching God that Tamim's entry into Ramallah be easy. I think of Radwa in Cairo holding her anxiety inside her only to carry it away with her, deliberately hidden and obscured, which makes it all the clearer to me.

Am I using this trance to escape the anxiety I feel about Tamim's entry? There would be nothing strange about that, given how cunningly the mind can work. Am I shifting the focus of my anxiety so I can bear it? Am I changing the direction of my thoughts to drive out my worries? The trick costs the soul nothing but surrender to this stream of consciousness.

From time to time I look at Tamim.

Tamim doesn't move his eyes from the window of the bus, through which he gazes at what he can see as though engraving the scenes on his memory.

"Baba, you were daydreaming," Tamim says to me as the bus starts moving. It sets off to cross the river in the direction of Palestine. A few minutes pass. We're close to the bridge now. "Now you'll see the bridge," I say to Tamim.

I've hardly finished this short sentence before we've crossed the bridge and put it behind us without Tamim noticing.

He turns to me in surprise—"Where's the bridge?"—and laughs out loud when I say to him, "It's a bridge shorter than a sentence."

I ask him to check our papers for the third or fourth time.

I look for the permit once again to be sure we haven't lost it and that the seals, stamps, signatures, and dates during which he is permitted to enter are correct.

This is the piece of paper that will allow Tamim the Palestinian to see Palestine.

Later, Tamim will say in an interview with London's *al-Hayat* newspaper that everything he saw after crossing the bridge he was seeing for the first time, so it was difficult for him to put a name to his feelings about it: "It was as though you'd put a microwave into the hands of a pre-Islamic poet like Imru' al-Qays."

Indeed, from this moment in his life onward, everything that twenty-one-year-old Tamim sees he will be seeing for the first time.

It will be the closing of one circle of life and the opening of another.

The Palestine of school books, stories, newspaper headlines, and CNN images will come to an end and the tangible Palestine will be born in his senses.

And I shall see how he sees everything.

I shall see, in a few days, how he receives his Palestinian identity card.

Will it be like the moment of his birth, on the banks of the Nile, twenty-one years ago?

Will it be like the moment when we chose his name?

Will he see a difference between it and the card they hung on his chest on the Malev aircraft when he traveled alone at the age of five and which the Hungarian flight attendant told him was his 'identity,' which they'd hung on his chest so that he wouldn't get lost?

A few minutes separate us from our encounter with the officers of Israel. A few minutes separate us from the faceless hyena of probabilities.

"You stand in the line. I'll keep my distance in the hall. I'll watch you till I'm sure you've got through safely and they haven't taken you for interrogation. I'll wait till then to present my papers."

Will he be subjected to that experience and its unknown outcomes on his first visit? Will he handle it properly? Will he get agitated and confused?

"If they call you for interrogation, only answer what you're asked. Remember it's your right to refuse to talk about politics. I'll be waiting for you in this hall no matter how late it gets. If they send you back, we'll go back together. After going through their control desk, you'll come out right into the baggage claim area. Take your bag. Leave the building immediately. Don't wait for me inside the building. Wait for me in the street."

He listens to me with the smile of a man whose family worries over him as though he were a child. I think to myself that Tamim is as anxious about me as I am about him, perhaps more so.

Such is the crossing point into Palestine.

The crossing point is the place where everyone is afraid for everyone else, a place of ambiguities that wear down the nerves. Here decisions are made that no one explains to you and procedures whose nature and extent you do not know are applied to you by human beings against whose authority there is no appeal. Here crouches a well-muscled, sharp-eyed wolf, a wolf that may leap at you with open jaws or pass you by to savage your neighbor in the line, when you barely have time to rejoice in your own escape before grieving that he has pounced on another. And you can't be sure he won't pounce on you until you're safely out of the place.

The crossing point nullifies the fatherhood of fathers, the motherhood of mothers, the friendship of friends, and the love of lovers. Here it is difficult to practice tenderness. Here the possibility of solidarity and rescue are negated. Here I can neither help my son nor protect him as a father.

Dictatorship, like the Occupation, nullifies fatherhood, motherhood, friendship, and love. I ask myself how many times do I have to feel powerless to protect the ones I love.

Now, as I return Palestine to Tamim, and Tamim to Palestine, I feel I'm surrendering him to the jailer.

Tamim's turn in the line gets one step closer. I watch him from a distance. I am now fearful, tranquil, disturbed, accepting, furious, joyful, sad, impotent, capable, apprehensive, annoyed, optimistic, pessimistic, calm, and agitated, as thoughts mix and combine in my imagination.

Every time the world throws me into the cage called 'waiting,' I know where to escape to.

I take my imagination, or let it take me, far from the cage.

My eyes are on Tamim as, step by step, he approaches the moment that will bring, or destroy, joy. I enter a maelstrom of fears and doubts.

I listen to my internal questions, which no one but I can hear. Stupid questions and wise questions follow one another as in a waking nightmare, or like the ghosts of questions. I follow after them; loud and low, wise and stupid, useful and trivial, contradictory, clear, and murky, they fluctuate between the serious and the absurd, as though a huge box of photos, new and old, had dropped from my hands, the photos falling in confusion on top of one another and turning into a jumble of projecting edges, colors, and sizes till they are no more than a blur of light and dark spots and ill-defined shadows. The questions run inside me, or I run behind them, between consciousness and unconsciousness, like one slowly emerging from anesthesia to find faces he doesn't recognize, or sinking into a stupor as the anesthetic starts to work inside his body. When will the waiting end, so that I can slip from between the jaws of this trap? Why am I certain life doesn't hold a single pure moment, and that each instant is like an alloy of moments that have fused together till they look, to the deluded and the naïve, like something pure and independent, though they are neither? Why is there always a thread of fear in the cloth of tranquility? Why does one enter a battle not because one is evil but because one is afraid? Why do I neglect a person when I am the one most concerned about him? Isn't it true that sometimes I show great patience for no better reason than that my patience has run out? Why do questions remain questions no matter how often men answer them?

I'm sure in my mind that Tamim will get in or we wouldn't have come here today.

I'm anxious about his getting in or I wouldn't have gone into the trance that just came over me.

Does our getting in deserve all this anxiety?

Doesn't my anxiety appear silly and embarrassing when compared to the chronic torments of my people? What does it matter whether we get in or are refused or arrested or even die here? Isn't the Palestinian surrounded by death? Aren't the torments he suffers at the borders and in the airports of the Arab dictatorships repeated and routinized to the point of banality? Can this trivial anxiety of mine be compared with the demolition of a house over the heads of those inside it in Jenin or Gaza? So what am I complaining about here? I want to make permanent history out of a passing trance. No one hears of us unless we're being bombarded by F-16 missiles or under the rubble of houses. We suffer a resounding and collective torment and let our screams out on the world's screens. We aren't just corpses and we didn't choose to be so. I want to deal with my unimportant feelings that the world will never hear. I want to put on record my right to passing anxieties, simple sorrows, small desires, and feelings that flare up briefly in the heart and then disappear. I don't say my anxiety is justified and I won't apologize for it. It's my anxiety and that's all.

I describe it as it is. I don't want anything from anyone. I don't pray for help or seek assistance or sympathy. All I want is to probe what is inside me so that I can know it, and listen for the voice of my soul and hear it. I want to write the history of things no one else will ever write for me. I want to carve the least of my feelings with a chisel on a stone next to the highway. I realize that I'm talking nonsense now, but it's been a brief fit, that's lasted only as long as it as taken me to smoke this cigarette.

I think about lighting another.

Suddenly I stop.

There he is. I see him now. I see Tamim. I see his right hand waving his papers at me over everyone's head. Then I see his face. His face at this moment is one big smile that would bring joy to any who sees it.

Tamim has got through. They haven't stopped him. They haven't interrogated him. They haven't sent him back to where he came from.

Tamim has got through.

The doctor insisted that the birth be natural no matter how long the wait. It was a cruel night in that small hospital on the bank of the Nile in June 1977. He didn't listen to our pleas for him to intervene, even if it meant a caesarean. The actual labor began at 3 p.m. but he went upstairs to sleep and left Radwa to suffer until just before dawn. The hospital was also his house, one floor of which he'd set aside for his living quarters, and he went up there to sleep. Radwa, who never complains, would scream with pain and then tell us, "I'm sorry," but before she could finish, the next cycle of pain would attack and her eyes would plead with the nurse, to no effect. I would take her hand and wipe the sweat off her cheeks and forehead with a handkerchief.

"I'm putting you to so much trouble. I'm sorry."

I looked at the faces of those with me in the room. What I saw there wasn't reassuring. The hours passed. The doctor didn't come. When he finally came, it was around six in the morning. He came, went in, and locked the door behind him.

We kept our eyes on a small, unlit, electric bulb over the door, a bulb that was covered with dust even though the hospital was new. I had been told it would light up red for a boy and green for a girl. As far as I was concerned, its light would be a signal that Radwa's long agony was over. When the red light came on, the nurse came out with the good news: "Congratulations, it's a lovely boy."

I push my way through the crowds in the passport hall toward him, my arms outstretched to meet his, which are opened as wide as they can go, holding his papers. I suddenly realize that he's almost as tall as I am. We hug. I pat his back. He pats mine. We spin around twice, three times, maybe four. Maybe we don't spin around at all and I just imagine it. Tamim has got through.

Now it's my turn.

I move to join one of the short lines to present my papers to the Israeli officer. Yes, Israeli. Otherwise, what would be the meaning of the Occupation?

Tamim refuses to enter the baggage claim area despite my firm instructions (when did children ever obey firm instructions? If it weren't for disobedience no child would ever grow up) and despite the fact that we have actually caught sight of his own suitcase on the conveyor belt in the neighboring hall. A moment later, mine appears too and he still can't be persuaded to go.

Tamim insists on waiting next to me to see what happens. I stop urging him and move slowly with the line. I say to myself, He too wants to be reassured.

I present my papers and wait.

47

He stands near me outside the line.

And he waits.

Four or five years later, on a recent visit, a teenage Israeli police-woman will confiscate the documents that I always present when on the bridge (my Palestinian ID, Israeli permit, and Jordanian passport), give me a small piece of paper with a few lines in Hebrew, and tell me in broken Arabic, "Wait there till you hear your name."

I wait about half an hour. I wait and it seems as though the time will never pass. We say 'time is precious' but I don't believe it. We often waste time of our own free will. In fact, we long for holidays and weekends and go out of our way to create opportunities to be lazy whenever we can, becoming experts at wasting time playing cards, watching television, and drifting from café to café. It isn't really the squandering of time that upsets people. What upsets them most, in my opinion, is having to wait to waste it.

One of the Occupation's crimes is to compel people to wait. To wait at crossing points, borders, and checkpoints. To wait while per-missions and permits are issued. To wait for the hours of opening and closing and of the curfew and its lifting. To wait for the hellish inter-rogation to end. To wait for the prison sentence to end. To wait for the electricity to come back on and for the water to come back on. To wait for all the dates and extensions to dates set for negotiation by the mysterious power that holds the Authority in its grip through the permanent concealing of its intentions. In addition and before all, to be forced to spend their lives waiting, year after year and generation after generation, for the Occupation itself to disappear.

I am still waiting for them to call my name.

They do not call it.

However, a fat soldier comes up to me and leads me quietly to the interrogation room.

A long row of seats in a narrow corridor.

Cameras sited conspicuously at the corners of the corridor and on the ceiling.

I sit down among the others who are already there—seven or eight persons of different ages, none of whom appears in the least worried and who wait in a wonderfully relaxed way, as though their presence here was completely natural and completely normal; as though they were waiting for a train that was about to arrive.

In front of us, closed doors.

We wait.

At first I feel miserable, but after a while I start laughing to myself at a funny story of Abu Sharif al-Sous's about waiting. In the old days, before Oslo and before the Authority, Israel used to grant one-month visit permits to people of the Bank living outside. Sharif Abu al-Sous came from Kuwait to Amman intending to go to the bridge the next day. He went to the Café Centrale in Amman and ordered himself a glass of tea. After waiting for a while, he called to the waiter and said with a laugh, "I asked for a glass of tea. Do me a favor and bring it before the permit runs out!"

I ask the one closest to me, "What happens inside?"

"The usual questions. Dumb questions. Don't worry about it."

After an hour and a half of waiting, I'm summoned to one of the rooms, where I find two people, one of whom, it turns out, will treat me pleasantly while the other treats me like an oaf—the traditional good cop/bad cop division of roles.

"Where are you going?"

"To Ramallah."

"Are you a member of the National Council?"

"An observer."

"Meaning?"

"Meaning I take part in the discussions but don't vote."

"Are you Fatah?"

"I'm independent."

"That's exactly what it says here."

"If you already know, why are you asking me?"

"You're here to answer questions, not ask them. It says too that you're a poet. Did you meet with writers from Israel outside? Did you meet with any Israelis outside?"

"I don't remember."

"What do you think of Abu Mazen?"

"I am on premises belonging to the security forces and do not wish to discuss politics."

"We just want to talk to an educated person like you, no more, no less. That's all there is to it."

"This is a border post, not a seminar room. You have my papers. If there's a problem with them, you can apply your procedures."

The silent colleague intervenes.

"Tea or coffee?"

I decline with a wave of my hand but he gets up, goes to another room, returns after two minutes, places a cup of tea in front of me, and leaves again. His colleague resumes his questions.

"Why don't you want to talk to me about politics?"

"Because of the lack of equality."

"What do you mean?"

"I mean that you're the stronger party. You have the power to allow me to enter, prevent me from entering, send me back to Amman, or send me to a prison in Israel and I have nothing, so what's the point in talking?"

"I can see you're angry even though things are looking good now. Arafat has appointed Abu Mazen prime minister, which means there's a chance of peace. What do you think of Abu Mazen?"

"Neither Abu Mazen nor anyone else will achieve anything because you'll never give him anything."

"How come?"

"Sometimes it seems to me you won't be happy till we appoint a Zionist as leader of the Palestinian people."

He smiles, then frowns.

"Who are you going to rely on in your obstinacy? If we expel you all to Egypt or Jordan, do you think Mubarak or Abdullah will care?"

The second interrogator re-enters.

"Where have you got to?"

"We've got to the threat of Transfer," I answer.

He gives a smirk so I go on with what I was saying: "Your colleague is threatening to throw the Palestinians into the sea."

"Transfer, my friend? The sea? The desert? Take me with you if they throw you out. It'd be better than going on the way we are now."

He looks at the glass of tea, notices that it remains untouched, but makes no comment. Then he surprises me by saying, "Anyway, you can go."

"That's it?"

"Goodbye."

Years after this interrogation session, the same thing will take place twice more. Since then, they've stopped calling me in, though I don't know how long this will last.

This time we don't have to wait long.

They don't take long to stamp my papers and I'm not called in for interrogation.

I've never needed good luck so much as I do today, having Tamim with me. I say to myself this is such good luck I can hardly believe it. It's difficult for a Palestinian to believe that he's having luck. It's my easiest entry to Palestine since I gained the right to do so two years earlier and has remained so for ten years. As to what may come later, who can be sure?

I leave the line, take Tamim's hand, and we enter the baggage claim area together happily, then exit onto the street. I hug him and he hugs me in a new embrace on soil he's standing on for the first time since Radwa gave birth to him twenty-one years ago.

Tamim's in Palestine.

3

The Yasmin Building

We reach the hill. We enter the Yasmin Building. The elevator takes us to the fifth floor. We go in, open the windows, and take from the chairs and couches the covers put there to protect them from the dust that gathers in Rafif's absence. I pick up the receiver of the ancient black telephone, make sure it's working, dial Cairo, and give the receiver to Tamim so he can speak to Radwa before I do. We pass the receiver back and forth. Our conversation seems to be made up of incomplete phrases and sentences. Radwa asks about our journey, we try to convey the details, and Tamim keeps saying, "Mama, I'm in Palestine."

Among other things I tell her, "Radwa, I want to say 'Thank you.'"

When I went to register his birth at the Ministry of Health in Egypt and have his birth certificate issued, I'd meant to write 'Jordanian' in the space for Father's Nationality, as in my passport. The only document I possess is one that proves that I'm a Jordanian; I didn't have one to present to the relevant official that proved I was Palestinian. Here Radwa intervened decisively: "Write 'Palestinian.'"

I wrote 'Palestinian.'

The official questioned it and I explained to him the history of the relationship between Palestine and Jordan, and that there was no such thing as a Palestinian passport now. He didn't ask too many questions, either because he was too good-hearted or because he didn't want to appear ill-informed. He accepted it and issued the certificate.

(Later, the word 'Palestinian' on this certificate will stand in the way of Tamim's right to obtain Egyptian nationality on the same basis as other children of Egyptian women married to non-Egyptians; for some unknown reason, Palestinians are excluded from that right.)

We call my mother in Amman and tell her of our safe arrival.

I turn on the water heater. We have to wait a while before we can bathe and change out of our traveling clothes.

I phone Husam to tell him we've arrived at the Yasmin apartment and he says, "I'm coming right over."

This is the second time I've spent a few days in elegant Rafif's elegant apartment, which contains her late grandfather, 'Omar al-Salih al-Barghouti's, furniture and a fragment of his library. She has added indoor plants and a modern kitchen, which leads straight out of the main room without a partition. Rafif lives in the apartment for a few days each year when she comes from Amman and has always insisted on giving me the keys when I come to Ramallah; she was especially insistent this time, so that Tamim and I could be comfortable.

Later, some years after this visit, Rafif will depart this life suddenly in Amman. She was starting her day at the offices of the magazine she edited when she collapsed. She never regained consciousness. I will receive the news by telephone in Cairo and travel to Amman immediately to be with my friend, her husband Dr. Muhammad Barakat. When he saw me, Muhammad's first words were, "She completed everything she set out to do, calmly and elegantly. She restored the family home in Deir Ghassanah, she furnished the apartment in the

Yasmin Building in Ramallah, she edited and published her grandfather's memoirs, held the finished book in her hands . . . and died."

Rafif al-Barghouti, who studied philosophy at the American University in Beirut, was one of the family's most elegant women, in language,
dress, and conduct. She designed the décor of her house herself with
a talent that made the simplest object stand out in its carefully chosen
spot. Unspoken mutual respect united us, as did a love of houseplants;
she made the balcony of her house in Amman a perfect garden, which
she tried to reproduce in the Yasmin Building even though she didn't
live there, leaving the key with Abu Hazim so that he could look after
the plants. The first thing I do at Rafif's house is to water these, which
are neglected even though Abu Hazim waters them whenever he can
gather the enthusiasm to walk here from his house in the Sharafa district.

I look for a piece of cloth, wet it, and clean the leaves of the plants
one by one, even the awkward fern. Then I go out onto the south-
facing balcony that is attached to the living room and water the plants
there too.

I call to Tamim to join me on the balcony but he doesn't answer.
I go into the living room and find him absorbed in reading a handwritten poem hung on the wall in an old wooden frame to the right of
the front door as you enter the apartment.

"Do you like it?"

"I'm still reading it."

"Leave it now and come with me. I want to show you something."

I take him out onto the balcony and ask him, "Do you see that arc
of buildings on the horizon?"

"What is it?"

"It's Jerusalem."

"Amazing. You could get to it on foot."

"You can get to it, my dear Mr. Tamim, with an Israeli permit only."

. . .

"When I was in the country two years ago, I refused to go there as an infiltrator. This time you and I will infiltrate."

"You have a plan?"

"We'll see."

"We have to."

We return to the living room and he starts reading over again, out loud:

You achieved, O 'Omar, all things in which men take pride,
So choose for your garb what exaltedness you may.
As for the land, its honor you defended
When evil men had led that honor astray.

I tell him, "I memorized it the last time I was here."

"What's the story behind it?"

"Ma'rouf al-Rusafi is praising 'Omar al-Salih al-Barghouti, Rafif's grandfather, after the British Mandate authority pardoned him and he returned from banishment."

"Which year?"

"1920."

"What did he do?"

"He took part in a demonstration in Jerusalem against Jewish immigration and the British Mandate, so the British banished him to Acre."

"Have you seen Acre?"

"I saw it for the first time last year."

I leave him standing, finishing al-Rusafi's poem, and stretch out on the couch.

The longing to relax after the tension of the journey makes me fall into a nap, or something like one. I find myself back in the only time I saw Acre, the summer before.

I was fifty-three years old that summer and had never been to Acre. The checkpoints weren't many at the time. Hikmat, my friend and host, said, "Come with me to Jenin. We'll spend a day and a night there, and then I'll show you Acre, Nazareth, Jaffa, and Haifa."

I stood on the walls of Acre. Immediately, a row of question marks lined up in front of me, all pointing the same way: "How was a city like this lost?"

A wall of dark presence, almost black in color. It curves with the beach, straightens out where the beach does, and curves again. Then you think it's disappeared but it returns to view. Towering. A battleship from below, from above it looks like an unlucky fishing boat. Wide. With the exaggeration to which the scene lends itself, I think, "If you played football on it, you'd think the ball would never fall into the sea or the city, but remain always on top" (of course it would fall, but the illusion was close to being real). What made me think of football in this historic place? Who would play with whom? Who would lose? Who would win? And was it a game I was thinking of or the war that a whole nation lost? At this point, I put my finger on an idea that struck my body full on, like a wave: Palestine didn't fall in a war that had a beginning and an end, like the wars we're familiar with. Wars big and small, from the Trojan War to the Vietnam War to the Second World War and more, begin and then end and you know, with a precision befitting the human mind, that you've lost or you've won. Then you think about what to do next and that's the end of it. But Jewish warships didn't come and bombard and breach this wall in an attack on the people of Acre. It's still here, where it always has been and as it always has been. No power besieged a Palestinian army, thus allowing it to raise the white flag and end everything with a final winner and loser. I think to myself Palestine was lost through drowsiness, slumber, and trickery. Every time we tried to wake up, we found death and cruel displacement to places of exile, to other pillows and to other mistakes—and yes, I do mean mistakes (and we're still making them). All this happened with a relentless slowness. How can an entire nation drowse? How could we have been so heedless—so heedless that our homeland became theirs?

Our enemy caught us at a moment of historic backwardness, as though we were incapable of realizing what would happen before it happened or at the moment it was happening, and perhaps we're still incapable of realizing it even now that it has happened. Or could it be that we did and do realize but are too weak to right the scales now that they've tilted? Will our scales stay tilted forever? For part of forever? Till when, exactly? It's unclear. As painfully unclear as a wolf's bite.

I think to myself, we didn't lose Palestine in war that we may now behave like the defeated and we didn't lose Palestine in a debate that we can get it back with proofs.

Our enemy caught us at the low point of our weakness, at the low point of our drowsiness.

We have the power now to tell our grandchildren that drowsiness will not be their lot forever, or even for part of forever.

We have the power to remind them of that strange proverb coined by our ancestors, "Had Acre feared the sea's roar, it would never have stood on the shore!"

All the same, we have to admit to them, and before them to ourselves, that we are responsible too. Our ignorance is responsible and our historical short-sightedness is responsible, along with our internal struggles, our tribal-familial logic, and the way we were let down by our Arab 'strategic depth,' which is made up of states enamored to the point of scandal with their colonizers. Nevertheless, we cannot take this as a reason to stay silent. We have to break the state of denial with which the world confronts us. We shall tell the tale the way it has to be told. We shall tell our personal histories one by one and shall recount our little stories as we have lived them and as our souls and eyes and imaginations remember them. We shall not let history be the history of great events, of kings and officers and books on dusty bookshelves. We shall recount what happened to us personally and the life stories of our bodies and our senses, which to the naïve will seem trivial, incoherent, and meaningless. The meaning is etched upon each individual woman, man, child, tree, house, window, and on every grave before which the national anthem will not be sung and which the historian's blind pen will not describe. We shall retell history as a history of our fears, our anxieties, our patience, our pillow lusts, and improvised courage. As a history of the making of an evening meal, of stories of love, innocent and otherwise, of emotions hidden from the grown-ups. As a history of the goat bombed by planes in its field and of the heroism of the child who peed in his pants out of fear but suddenly felt brave and stood, wide-eyed, before the long dark line of tanks. As a history of our secret and public desires, of our jokes and our laughter, of "a wink from her eye at the wedding and the boy went crazy." A history of all the journeys we have made and all the distances we have crossed or been forbidden to cross and of every straightforward, ordinary trip between two cities or two situations. A history of our making fun of our leadership and our mockery of their decorations, medals, and military ranks. A history of the obstinacy of our bodies and of our souls, no record of which is to be found in archives or registries. We shall make the two-hour electricity cuts to our houses important events because they are important events. We shall make the glance of the child at his friend's empty desk in Class Four a chapter in his workbook on the living and the dead. We shall enter in the records a story of love destroyed by soldiers, or the head of the family, or the stupidity of the lovers themselves, so as to draw the world's attention to the loss of a love story that concerns the world. I shall record our sitting on the wall of Acre and eating a meal of fish in Christo's restaurant like any tourist who has come from far away. I shall record the history of this fish meal too, and here I am, writing it. I shall make of every feeling that ever shook my heart an historic event and I shall write it.

From Acre we headed straight for Nazareth and Haifa, but before reaching these we went by the house of Ahmad al-Shuqayri, a native of Acre who lost his city in the Nakba of 1948. A refugee, he obtained an education and became a lawyer. The first chairman of the Palestinian Liberation Organization died, however, without seeing Acre again, as liberator, visitor, or tourist, and was laid to rest in Amman.

At the Church of the Annunciation in Nazareth, we found ourselves at the heart of our history, in the midst of a group of tourists from Japan, most of them nuns. We were coming full circle. I said to Hikmat, "Let's be Japanese tourists today. This place will be ours for an hour or so, and then we'll leave." I told myself that I'd write the history of these seconds during which I felt I was a Japanese tourist. I thought, I wish Tawfiq Zayyad were alive so that I could visit him in this city of his that he never left and whose mayor he was for many years. I thought, did the communist poet really have to go by car to Jericho to congratulate Arafat on his return to the homeland, only to be killed in a traffic accident on the way back? He thus deprived us all of his wit and his patriotic poems that we learned by heart as children, and also of his valiant deeds in the Knesset, where he raised his fist in the faces of Shamir, Sharon, and Netanyahu, clenched it hard, and shouted in Hebrew, "You want to throw me out of the session because I've got you all by the balls. By the balls, you child killers!"

The guards dragged him out of the chamber to his unceasing stream of insults. I saw the scene when it was picked up by the television stations. I thought, I'll write this poet as he clenches his fist and bawls, knowing that it makes no difference—and here I am doing so.

We left the city of Nazareth like the Japanese tourists. We got into the car and set off for Jaffa and Haifa—Jaffa, the city that liberated the

Mediterranean from its long name when the Palestinians decided that 'the Sea of Jaffa' was enough.

Haifa, though, is the city that imagination built as it wanted and as all cities would want to be built. To climb to the top of Mount Carmel and look out over the city and its sea is to climb to the meaning of beauty. I climbed Carmel and thought, now I am in it, I am in Haifa, this 'beautiful city.' Say that and nothing more. And I will say nothing more.

It seems Tamim thought I'd dropped off. He'd gone inside, taken a shower, and was waiting to hear my plan, still examining 'Omar al-Salih al-Barghouti's old furniture, his black telephone, his salon set which had been so splendid in its day, and a part of his library.

Later, his book *Marahil* (Stages), a huge work containing his memoirs from the end of the nineteenth century to the year of his death in Ramallah in 1965, will be published and I will buy a copy at the Cairo Book Fair. The second part of *Marahil* consists of political memoirs covering the period of the British Mandate over Palestine and the political, party-based, cultural, and educational work undertaken in an attempt to save it from the Zionist plan that aimed to establish a state for the Jews on the rubble of our cities and villages. These are memoirs from the pen of a lawyer well-versed in political analysis. The first part, however, is devoted to the family and the village of Deir Ghassanah. It is full of vaunting and boasting about everything to do with the Barghouti family, which the head of the family comes close to canonizing and whose every distinguishing characteristic he takes pains to record, as though it were God's Chosen Family. Soon enough, however, he forgets himself and describes how the same family oppressed women and the weak that lived around them. He recounts, for example, how the Barghoutis would send the nawar (gypsies) who lived on the edges of Deir Ghassanah to do compulsory Ottoman military service in place of the sons of the family, and that the family owned slaves, which was "something natural at the time," and that poor members of the family used to walk with a "sloping shoulder" indicating that they performed manual labor to support their families when in general the Barghoutis didn't need to do any physically demanding work. If a man passed a woman, she was not allowed to keep on walking; she was supposed to squat on her haunches until the man had gone and then continue on her way. He also boasts of the Barghoutis' clothes because "the Barghoutis had pockets" while the peasants in the other villages put their money either in their head coverings or their belts. I read what he has to say in praise of the pocket:

> Villagers put many of their belongings in their head gear, between their skull caps and their tarbushes. If one of them is wearing a kufiya with a rope retainer he places his papers and his money in his belt. Thus they use their head covering or their belts as places to keep things. The Barghouti, however, used to view this as shameful and would put his belongings in his pockets. A member of the family once told me that a large number of village headmen were summoned by the governor of Jerusalem, who told them to put their seals to an official document. All of them pulled their seals out from their belts, except for the headman of Deir Ghassanah, whose seal was in his pocket. "Are you a Barghouti?" the governor asked him, to which the man replied, "That I am!"

I laughed for a long time over this paragraph and mentioned it to my friends. It became a common habit of theirs to accost me whenever we met with the mocking question, "Do you have pockets, Mourid?"

I'd complete the exchange for them by answering, "Then you must be a Barghouti!"

I go inside to take a shower and change my clothes.

Anis, Husam, and Abu Ya'qoub come and we go together to have lunch at Abu Hazim's. Afterward I take Tamim on a tour of Ramallah and al-Bireh and he is amazed at how the two cities intermesh. The right side of a street may be in al-Bireh while the left falls in Ramallah. I take him to al-Manara, the Ramallah Secondary School, Batn al-Hawa and the Church of God, the Friends' School for Boys and the Friends' School for Girls, Ziryab's Café, Rukab's ice cream parlor, Ramallah Municipality Public Library, the Arts Center, the Qasaba Theater and cinema, the Sakakini Cultural Center, and Shari' al-Iza'a.

"In the fifties we used to call it Lovers' Lane."

"It doesn't look like that now. Where are the lovers? Where are the girls? Where are the trees?"

"It seems everything goes backward everywhere."

"It seems Ramallah's like today's Cairo—a 'city of Islamic law.'"

"The boys and girls from the secondary schools—Ramallah, the Friends, the Hashimiya, and so on—used to take their strolls here in the afternoons and on the weekends, promenading and making dates. They were experts in the art of flirting and attracting attention in all its forms. Stories of love, both dumb and fantastic, were born here. Scandals, embarrassments, and . . . ."

"Normal life, in other words."

In the evening, we eat at al-Bardouni's. We agree to meet Husam the following morning to arrange our 'infiltration' into Jerusalem. At night, Tamim and I go back to the Yasmin Building. We go out onto the balcony. Jerusalem looks like a great crescent of lights crowning the quiet of the night.

Half asleep and half awake, I return as a boy a little younger than Tamim is now to the nearby school with the arches. I wonder, was I less in pain in those days than he is? The place was mine and my body was free in a free city that knew no dour looks and had yet to acquire the strict moralistic atmosphere in which Cairo, and all Arab cities, live today. At Cairo University, the beautiful cafeteria has been torn down and all the other cafeterias in Egyptian universities have been closed so that the students can't socialize between lectures. As a result, there's no place left to talk about politics and no place left for stories of love. Ninety per cent of the girl students wear the headscarf or the face veil—from religious belief, to fit in, because they've been preached at, out of poverty, or by contagion.

In that dreamy space where the world had the feel of velvet and the taste of peaches, and the lusts of adolescence shot sparks from my growing body, I'd go during the day with my friends to the city's gardens, cafés, and parks. If one of us got to know a girl, we'd hide our pounding hearts from our families. We'd lie to get out of homework so we could go out and exchange visits and small gifts on our birthdays and dance and have fun and commit small stupidities.

At night, almost every night, I turned to poetry, writing and erasing, or to the short story, writing and tearing up, or to drawing with a pencil, never keeping anything I'd done.

On mornings during term time, everything about school was inviting, because it was a wider society than that of the house and there was nothing to spoil it apart from the math exam and Muhammad Basala.

Basala was top of the class each year and I'd be second and each year this got on my nerves when the final results were announced because I couldn't think of any reason why my final mark should always be one lower than his. Things continued like that until one year I got first place and Basala got second. I took my friends to the cinema in celebration of this coup and we saw *The King and I* with Yul Brynner at the Cinema Dunya, though we didn't take any of it in because we were more interested in the Ramallah girls around us in the elegant theater. Falling in love, a possibility in Ramallah, acted on my body and soul as much as a love fulfilled would have done. Our adolescence passed in a state of infatuation with the world, music, pictures, colors, of the first rain in September and the first snow on the hills, as well as of gratitude to any family that might visit ours bringing their daughter with them. We experimented with all the different ways of showing interest—gentleness and aggressiveness, calculated neglect and going too far, displays of shyness and claims of experience and multiple relationships, and always we wanted to appear older than we were. The girl would try out all her weapons at one go—bashfulness and openness, retreat and advance, closing all doors and then leaving them a little ajar—and when she walked on Shari' al-Iza'a, I'd feel she could see me walking behind her through the back of her head without turning around and would adjust the rhythm of her steps as the fancy took her, hurrying up or slowing down according to her whim, sending silent messages of encouragement or rejection. This in itself was enchanting.

The discovery of the body and its pleasures opened the door to infatuation with life and its small sins and our ambitions for it, both fanciful and realistic.

Mousa 'Abd al-Salam dreamed of buying an oud so that he could play the tunes of our common idol, Farid al-Atrash.

'Omar Dhib dreamed of having of a proper camera to hang over his shoulder so that he could stroll through the streets looking like a foreign tourist.

'Adel al-Najjar and Fuad Tannous collected Beatles records so that they could hold parties with them.

Rami al-Nashashibi and Basim Khouri never stopped playing practical jokes.

We were good students and would join the demonstrations in support of Algeria and express our love for Nasser, Lumumba, Castro, and Ho Chi Minh. We followed with boundless enthusiasm the news of the unification of Egypt and Syria and the birth of the United Arab Republic, the first in our modern history, and we mourned its subsequent breakup. Later, we were overjoyed by the socialist transformation taking place in Nasser's Egypt and took part in demonstrations demanding total Arab unity. We dreamt of traveling to universities, completing our education, and returning to work, help our families, and become, one day, good boys.

This Ramallah that I recall in my imagination is just a mirage now. It isn't the Ramallah that I'm showing Tamim today. It's as if it, along with Cairo, Beirut, Damascus, and all the other Arab cities, had been a creation of our imaginations, not a reality. Satellite-channel sheikhs and Islamic fundamentalists say that lands were lost and defeats suffered one after the other because of our generation's dissoluteness and distance from religion. The same people hated Nasser, hated Arab unity, hated socialism, and hated our whole generation. I can't understand these charges at all. Here, simply, was a city that decorated its streets for holidays, girls and boys who walked through its spaces, and records whose music we listened to obsessively, our hearts pounding with what we thought was love. We, in their view, are the cause of the defeat.

Tamim's world is not like mine when I was his age. I walk with him along Lovers' Lane and realize that nothing is as it was. The street, politics, political parties, religion, love, money, visits, school, left and right, women's clothes, people's thoughts, party politics—they've all changed so much that we seem to be living in a different era. Only someone unconscious of the world around him could claim now to experience that delicious daze in which the world has the feel of velvet and the taste of peaches.

I'm not saying that the city's past was brilliant. There was poverty. There was the pervasive presence of the Jordanian secret police and the persecution of the nationalist parties and figures. The Nakba was ever-present in people's eyes, even if they turned aside to their small pleasures. Since the loss of Palestine, we no longer have a garden of only roses. Pain is in every pleasure, a snake in every crack.

I do not weep for any past. I do not weep for this present. I do not weep for the future. I live through my five senses, trying to understand our story, trying to see. I try to hear a lifetime of voices. I try sometimes to tell the story and I don't know why; perhaps because the history books will never write what I write.

I start the morning by phoning Abu Saji. I wake Tamim. We get to the office on time.

I show him Tamim's papers and his pictures of the required size and leave him to fill in a form for a Palestinian identity card.

Husam joins us to take us in his car to Jerusalem in an adventure that may or may not succeed. When he notices my anxiety, he says, "We'll see what it's like at the checkpoint. If there are a lot of people waiting, it means they're checking permits carefully. If so, we turn around and go back the way we came before we get to the soldiers."

"There's no other way?"

"There's no other way."

"Wouldn't it be better to go in a car with yellow Israeli number plates?"

"Let's try today and if we fail, I'll arrange things with 'Sam.' He has yellow plates."

We go. It's the first scenario. The jam of cars at the Qalandya barrier is a bad sign. Husam takes us back to Ramallah. We have lunch with Marwan al-Barghouti and dinner at Za'rour's restaurant.

Next day we go to see Sam, setting off with greater optimism this time, though the anxiety hasn't entirely dispersed. I enjoy Sam's company and I like his personality, which combines intelligence with kindness and a careful choice of words whatever the subject. We join the long line of those waiting and move forward meter by meter toward the ultimate moment of tension.

We reach the barrier.

The Israeli soldier looks casually at our faces and gestures for us to pass without asking for anyone's ID. Tamim jumps off his seat with joy, kisses Sam's head, and thanks him.

In Arabic but with the accent of people from al-Bireh born in America, Sam answers, "Tamim, you are now at the gates of Jerusalem."

Before entering the city, we stop to buy any camera that will do the job (just like any tourists). We arrive at the Damascus Gate.

How small that Israeli soldier seems, standing with his machine gun inside an aperture at the top of the ancient, lofty wall. I think he's on his own here, but now he's turned into many soldiers. In each of the wall's openings is a soldier and at the side of the steps leading to the gate are more soldiers, their fingers stuck to their triggers as though the guns had come straight from the factory like that. Their eyes are fixed on us, even though their forefathers gave them to understand that they'd set up their state on a land without a people, a land in which there were no Arabs and which had no owner. In the street itself are police cars, their teams, also armed, sitting in them or standing beside them.

Tamim dashes into a telephone kiosk in the street and calls Radwa in Cairo.

"Mama, I'm in Jerusalem. I'm at the Damascus Gate. Baba and I are in Jerusalem."

I watch Tamim in the telephone kiosk. I see him in Radwa's arms, right after she left the Dr. Gohar Maternity Hospital. She is standing on the bank of the Nile directly in front of the hospital gate in a light summer dress with a pattern of small roses, holding Tamim in her arms and looking at him. He is only two days old and his eyes are closed against the mid-June sun but he isn't asleep. Our car is waiting to take us home after becoming mother, father, and son. The son has a name that has been entered in the records, ledgers, and statistics of the government. The name is his and denotes him but the son doesn't know it. He hasn't joined society or a sect or a creed yet. At the moment, he is a life in process of formation, a life that seeks air and milk and warmth and sleep so that it can wake from its slumber and seek again what it has obtained day after day, and so on until new demands grow within it. He is as yet unaware of the borders between countries whose crossing causes us such misery. He doesn't know the meaning of the watches we wear on our wrists. He is life in a small body and a soul that is slowly building itself. But wherever this small body goes, and wherever we go, its name is now "son of Mourid and Radwa," and our names are now "Umm Tamim" and "Abu Tamim."

"Photograph us here, Mourid, and get the Nile in the picture."

At our home in Mohandiseen, I'd started training myself in how to carry Tamim properly in my arms. I was just getting the hang of it and was learning some of the sounds and movements that would make him notice me or produce a smile or a laugh, when the Egyptian government expelled me. It expelled our family relationship, it expelled our way of living, it expelled our marriage, and it expelled the possibility of us, Radwa and me, raising the new child together.

I was a companion to his childhood, and he to my fatherhood, for only five months and five days. I was away from him for seventeen years, during which I saw him at widely separated intervals.

His first birthday came as I started my first year in exile around the world. I mailed him a birthday present in a small envelope. It was a poem entitled 'Tamim' and dated 13 June 1978.

He grew, sheltering in his beauty, and slowed my fear
But longing hastened my desire.
And I would speak truly if I said the windows

And the light and the grass resemble him
And that the poems cannot catch up with him
For he keeps running and rising
While poetry walks on two crutches.

We go through the Damascus Gate to the relatively shady Khan al-Zeit market. We make our way with difficulty through the market, which is crowded with passersby and buyers and sellers. We see few foreign tourists. Israel has succeeded in designing routes for tourists that stick to the Jewish bazaars that were erected after the occupation of the city in 1967. The result is that the tourist comes to Old Jerusalem and leaves again without discovering that there is an Arab quarter that is stuffed with bazaars and shops selling curios and necklaces and carved Christian and Islamic objects. This has destroyed the Arab Jerusalemites' primary economic resource. We pass Zalatimo's Sweets and Ja'far's Kanafeh but Tamim prefers to buy, rather than kanafeh, a piece of sweet semolina pastry.

We keep going in the direction of the Via Dolorosa.

It amazes me that I am now walking in the city as a father, when half a century before I walked in it as a son, and that now my son walks beside me.

I ask myself, is his Jerusalem my Jerusalem or something different? I saw it as a child and as an older man, and it was lost to me in between. Tamim is starting to get to know it now as a young man.

I come to it after absence and find myself comparing stone with stone and matching street with street and my school as it is now with my school as it was then and looking for my favorite shoe shop. I was very concerned to buy shoes that would please the teenage girls in Rukab's Garden on Sundays, or a real wool jersey that would spare my mother long evenings with two exhausting knitting needles. In the here and now, Tamim rubs the stone of the road against the stone

70

of imagination. He compares the reality of the mosque, the church, the crosses and the crescents with his images of them derived from the delight of narration, from colored books, statistics, and the magic of naming. He counts the ancient gates to confirm with his eyes the accuracy of what his ears had heard from the storyteller, who was me. Now he is inside the narrated scene—the narrated scene as it is in real life, needing no one to describe it. But, I tell myself, no reality cancels out imagination. Reality waylays us quickly but gives rise in the mind to further imagining. I come close to asking myself if there is a 'truth' outside the human 'imagination,' and am at loss for an answer.

I don't know if I was right to be so surprised when Tamim asked me to take a photograph of him beneath the street sign on which *Tariq al-Alam* is written in Arabic and under that in Latin characters *Via Dolorosa*, with two words in Hebrew at the top. It would never have occurred to me that I would stop to take a photo here or anywhere else in Jerusalem. Everything was fixed in place and secure and natural, like my own presence there. The steps of Christ along the Via Dolorosa from the Lions Gate to the Church of the Resurrection were just one of the facts and features of the city, like the weather, the trees, and the ancient walls. The Via Dolorosa was just a street we used, a narrow street in which we took care of our affairs and did our shopping or which we went down on our way to the one next to it. All the sacred sites nearby with their names, and the minarets, mosques, churches, crosses, bells, columns, domes, and tombs of the sultans and saints to which these alluded, were the ordinary and familiar that was always where it always had been, to whose destiny and significance I gave no thought. 'History' was a street, a shop, sweets, shoes, schools, stubborn weeds on walls, teenagers' quarrels, and lusts, attainable or unattainable—not a landmark where photos are taken. Taking pictures was the Japanese, European, and American tourists' and pilgrims' 'thing,' not our 'thing.'

71

The narrow road takes us on a slight curve to the covered market. Then two Arab guards stop us at a small door. They've spotted the camera in Tamim's hand.

"Tourists?"

"No, we're from here."

"Welcome. Go on in."

We go through the door.

Suddenly, a burst of light fills the horizon. We forget the narrow, dark streets. It's as though we've been transported to a newly discovered planet.

The sky lies stretched out at full length, as though it had woken up full of energy to start its morning, leaving some of its white pillows lying around forgotten in the form of clouds scattered randomly over its celestial bed sheet.

This is the Dome of the Rock.

Stand, stranger, in its shadows.

Take it in with all your senses.

Think of the fact that today it is you who is the stranger.

You are a stranger to it—you, its son, its rightful owner; you who, by virtue of eye and of memory, of documents and of history, of inscriptions, colors, trees, Qur'anic verses, poems, and aged tombstones, are its possessor.

Stand, stranger, and look:

This is the Dome of the Rock.

The daylight spreads its gold over the golden dome, whose vast crescent and octagonal walls are inscribed with ancient blue, with the supplications of pilgrims and the exhalations of those who pray.

The al-Aqsa Mosque and the Dome of the Rock stand side by side. Around and between them are centuries-old cypresses, eucalyptuses, palms, and other trees whose names I don't know. To our right we see worshipers entering and exiting the mosque as they have done for hundreds of years. Everything is as it always has been except for the Occupation, as a result of which the Palestinian's ability to pray here has become a dream that goes beyond religious prescriptions to become a political 'struggle' too.

Today Tamim's dream comes true. He performs a prayer of greeting to the two mosques. He wants his prayer to be recorded in his personal history here in this place whose habit it is to call out to the five senses of those who see it, "Don't slacken here for an instant. Don't slacken here, senses. Do your duty to the full now. Do your job as well as you possibly can. Go everywhere. Smell, see, touch, taste. Learn how history becomes stone and identity a building."

Tamim doesn't take photos or ask me to take his; without anyone saying anything, we seem to have decided that the camera would turn us into tourists forever. We have thrown it into the nearest waste basket. Yet, just like one-day tourists, we have hurried on to the Church of the Resurrection and the Mosque of 'Omar that stands beside it, built at the spot where the Caliph 'Omar ibn al-Khattab prayed on entering Jerusalem, refusing to pray in the Church the Resurrection in case later on the Muslims made his having prayed there an excuse to turn it into a mosque. He wished to demonstrate his respect for the church and to make sure that the Muslims who came after him would respect it as such forever. He wanted it to remain a Christian church. As a result, its 'old' cross stands alongside the 'new' crescent to this day.

Jerusalem has tired us. By 'us' I mean all humanity. I can't think of a city on the face of the planet that has tired the world's people as has Jerusalem. A city that refuses to be a city, land that refuses to be land. How can this be when the sacred has piled up here, in it, on it, and around it, layer upon layer, throughout the ages? Perhaps it was land before people became fully aware of what their world looked like, before news of God had reached us, before it had been trodden by the leather-strapped sandals of the prophets, walking their steps of faith. Perhaps it was land once, but with all this sanctity it has become, unfortunately, a piece of the heavens. Here the sacred has acquired the fluidity of clouds, of meaning, of imagination, to the point that the stones have lost their stone-ness, the streets their street-ness. The roof-ness of the roofs and domes has taken wing and the buildings are now roofed with meanings. Interpretations pile high but no sooner are they seized by the mind, hoping for clarification, than they are pushed aside by the hand of obscurity. Jerusalem's solidity has turned into the fluidity of supplications and prayers. Even this heavy, towering, dark wall that surrounds it seems to come from an ancient dream that repeats itself every time a believer passes through its arches and gates, a dream that the new arrival is destined to live and the departing traveler is urged never to forget. Horses have crawled to it on wounded knees squealing beneath the long-ings of riders prepared to die. Temple after temple has been built in it as an abode for the soul of man. And it has risen and risen, year after year, century after century, until it has become inseparable from the sky; and Jerusalem wants to remain sky, and as mysterious and ambiguous as the sky.

But Jerusalem is land.

And it is occupied land.

Land, and occupied by a powerful army whose only purpose is to keep my body, voice, steps, and memory far from it and stop me forever from reaching it. The world isn't souls and clouds. The world is states, soldiers, borders and passports, visas and electronic searches, building laws and taxes, residence permits and cars that run on petrol, not prayers. Only the policeman now has the power to let us pray or stop us doing so. The Israeli policeman is now the master of the city, or desires to be. It is the armed policeman who organizes and decides, not the heavens or amulets, not the grief of those who have lost it or the prayers of those who love it.

Jerusalem is a city like any other city.

"Since when has Jerusalem been a city like any other city?" you ask me and I answer, "Since the soldiers in it came to outnumber its holy sites a thousand times over."

From that ancient day on which it chose to be celestial, the soldiers have decided to love it by brandishing their weapons in the face of history.

Jerusalem has been a city like any other city from the day walls and checkpoints were built around it, from the day it became filled with government centers, police goons, surveillance cameras on electricity poles, nationality laws, police stations, army camps, torture sessions, and conquerors who dance to celebrate the day they conquered it instead of their own anniversaries.

Jerusalem has been a city since it was forbidden to us.

I told Tamim, "I'll take you to Orient House."

A beautiful, haughty villa. A very earthly mansion, built by builders using their worldly muscles who drank a lot of tea and complained of the cold, the heat, and the poor wages, as they would with any other block of apartments, house, and shop on man's earth.

In Orient House, the late Faisal al-Husseini carried on his functions as manager of the city and representative of the PLO. Here Jerusalem's guests—tsars, kings, ambassadors—were once received and moved through its elegant foyers. Here are offices for maps and statistics overseen by Khalil al-Tafakji, the most prominent Palestinian expert on settlement policies and the attempts to Judaize the city through the expulsion of its Arab inhabitants. (Israel had yet to issue its decree closing Orient House and all other PLO offices in Jerusalem.)

We went and talked to Khalil al-Tafakji, who appears to know the history of almost every building and house in Jerusalem by heart. Tamim asked him if he could look over some maps for academic research and al-Tafakji had what he wanted copied. Tamim started to explain what else he needed for the research.

Al-Tafakji, with the scholarly decisiveness that I admire in him, told him, "Ask me short, specific questions, to save time."

Later, the Israeli army will raid Orient House and the government of Israel will decide to close it and all other buildings from which any Palestinian activity is managed, arguing that Jerusalem doesn't belong to the Palestinians. Protests, sit-ins, and demonstrations demanding its reopening erupt but achieve nothing and it remains closed until further notice.

From Orient House, we go to an exhibition of hand-painted porcelain and ceramics run by a family that came originally from Turkey to restore the decorative work on the Haram al-Sharif and stayed on in Jerusalem. We buy beautiful dishes, an electric lamp with an oval base of porcelain hand-painted in shades of blue with designs of foliage and green roots, and a similarly painted flower vase as gifts for Radwa in Cairo. And yes, in Jerusalem, the people of God's city buy and sell dinner plates, shirts, fruit, shoes, socks, flowers, pickles, new cars, kitchen appliances, bank shares, tins of sardines, lottery tickets, and sandawitshat (I don't want to call them shata'ir; I don't like the word, or most of the new words proposed by the Arabic Language Academy).

At the end of our stolen 'tourist' visit to Jerusalem, and again like one-day tourists, we have dinner in the garden of an old Palestinian restaurant and from there set off to return to Ramallah.

The Israeli army doesn't stop us at the checkpoint.

Leaving Jerusalem is permitted—very permitted, in fact, and at any hour. If it weren't, how could its Judaization and the cleansing of its Arab inhabitants take place?

Leave the road of departure forever open. Keep the road of return forever closed. Otherwise, what would be the meaning of the Occupation?

Before, Tamim had seen Jerusalem through my eyes and through stories. Today, for the first time, he has seen it with his own eyes. Now it belongs to him.

I don't know what of Jerusalem settled in his eyes forever and have no way to write of that. A few years later though, he will let all of Palestine know, when he writes his poem 'In Jerusalem,' which will become the most famous poem about the city in Arabic that I know of.

I Was Born There
I Was Born Here

The Occupation stretched the distance between Tamim and Deir Ghassanah to more than twenty-one years, his whole life till then. Tamim took a large step when we obtained his permit, and the distance started to shrink. Now only twenty-seven kilometers separate Tamim from Deir Ghassanah. He knows that I was born 'there.' In half an hour I'll be saying to him, "I was born here."

I'm not a politician, but the Occupation distorts and destroys things that affect me personally and affect others whom I know and love. Occupation, like dictatorship, doesn't just corrupt political and party life but the lives of individuals too, even individuals who have nothing to do with politics. One of the Occupation's cruelest crimes is the distortion of distance in the individual's life. This is a fact: the Occupation changes distances. It destroys them, upsets them, and plays with them as it likes. Whenever the soldiers kill someone, the customary distance between the moments of birth and death is distorted. The Occupation closes the road between two cities and makes the distance between them many times the number recorded on the maps. The Occupation throws my friend into prison and makes the distance between him and his living room one to be measured in years and in the lives of his sons and daughters, who will give him grandchildren he will never see. The Occupation pursues a fugitive in the hills and makes the distance between sleep and his pillow one to be measured in the howling of wolves and the darkness of caves, while the leaves of trees become his only dining table. It teaches him how to turn his shoes and the stones into a pillow beneath his head, above which dreams and nightmares interweave. The soldier at the checkpoint confiscates my papers because he doesn't like the look of me for some reason and the distance between me and my identity becomes the distance between his pleasure and his displeasure. The soldier of the Occupation stands on a piece of land he has confiscated and calls it 'here' and I, its owner, exiled to a distant country, have to call it 'there.'

Many of my friends around the world express surprise at this Palestinian attachment to place of origin and concern for family ties. Some even scoff at it and contrast it with their own open-armed acceptance of adventure, discovery, a nomadic lifestyle and residence in places that they choose and change according to their fancy, without the slightest regret at leaving family or even homeland behind. They remind me that the world is wider and more beautiful than 'our villages' and 'our families.' I understand this beautiful sense of the vastness of the world. Like them, I love movement, journeys, and living in new places. What these friends forget is that it is they who choose to distance themselves. They are the ones who take the decisions and make the plans and then present their passports (recognized everywhere) and get on planes and trains and cars and motorcycles and go to places where three conditions that the Palestinian cannot meet are fulfilled: first, that it is their preference and choice to go to specifically these places; second, that these places always welcome them; and third and most important, that it is in their power to return to their home country whenever they desire and decide. The Palestinian forced to become a refugee, to migrate, and to go into exile from his homeland in the sixty years since the Nakba of 1948, or the forty since the June 1967 War, suffers miseries trying to obtain a document by which he will be recognized at borders. He suffers miseries trying to obtain a passport from another state because he is stateless and has to go through Kafkaesque interrogations before being granted an entry visa to any place in the world, even the Arab states. The Palestinian is forbidden to enter his own country by land, sea, or air, even in a coffin. It is not a matter of romantic attachment to a place but of eternal exclusion from it. The Palestinian stripped of an original identity is a palm tree broken in the middle. My foreign friends have control over the details of their lives but a single Israeli soldier can control the details of the life of any Palestinian. This is the difference. This is the story.

Anis comes to pick us up in his car.

He doesn't keep us waiting long. He's our cousin and is regarded with affection by the whole family. We suggest Tamim sit in the front next to Anis so that he can see as much as possible of the road, and I sit next to Husam and Ya'qoub in the back. Ya'qoub is the grandson of Abu Hazim—a talented boy who is studying the qanun, or Arab zither, and memorizes popular songs, some of which he sings to us.

We set off northward, in the direction of Deir Ghassanah.

Anis and Husam keep up a constant stream of anecdotes about the family and we laugh the whole way.

Anis keeps busy telling Tamim about the villages and places that we pass:

"This is Surda" (the Surda checkpoint hasn't been set up yet).

"This is the leper colony."

"This is Birzeit University."

"The street on your right goes to Kobar."

"Soon we'll be at the 'Atara checkpoint."

"Get your IDs ready."

ID cards in hand, we arrive at the checkpoint.

The first Israeli soldier doesn't stop us. He is clearly an Ethiopian Jew belonging to the Falasha, whose exit from Ethiopia was arranged by Israel several years ago in connivance with Ja'far al-Nimeiry, then president of Sudan. The second soldier, a European Jew who looks like a film star, waves us through without checking or asking any questions; in fact, he seems to me to smile at us as he waves his hand. We are delighted, because the 'Atara checkpoint is the only one between Ramallah and Deir Ghassanah, meaning that from here on our way is clear. I think to myself that Tamim is lucky.

Husam says, "Your road is blessed, Tamim. Everything will be straightforward from now on, God willing. If 'Atara's 'moving,' everything's fine."

Anis says with confidence, "They know my car. That's why they didn't stop you."

"It has red number plates too, meaning it's a government car, a car belonging to the Authority," says Ya'qoub.

"Are they such good friends with the Authority?" asks Tamim.

Anis answers, "Not friends, but they look out for us. One of the benefits of Oslo, of which your dad doesn't approve."

"They look out for you because you look out for them."

"What's wrong with that?"

"That's not how the homeland is supposed to relate to the Occupation."

"I suggest we continue this discussion, Mr. Mourid, the day we bring you an independent state. I don't know what you'll have to say then."

"I'll say to you then what the poet Ilya Abu Madi said."

"What's that?"

"He said 'I know not.'"

Anis laughs. He understands from this sarcastic answer that I wish to put an end to political discussion.

Our cousin Anis is a good-hearted Fatah activist, with a clean conscience and clean hands. He has never sought to benefit from his friendship with Yassir Arafat or his heartfelt defense of him and of the Fatah leadership at all times, though it would be easy for him to do so. We used to tell him that his support for the Fatah leadership was 'romantic.' Then we raised it to 'Sufi-like.' Then we raised again it to 'a matter of faith.' Then we raised it to 'blind.' He never allows anyone to criticize Fatah in general or Arafat in particular in his presence. We continue on our way, exchanging funny family stories and laughing all the time, as though on a weekend picnic.

Anis resumes his commentary: "On your left is the settlement of Halamish. Every day they add a building, so now it stretches all the way to the hill next to it. After that is the village of Beit Rima. Then . . . the capital."

He means, of course, the capital of the Barghoutis, Deir Ghassanah. No Barghouti misses an opportunity to talk, with pride naturally, of the family and of Deir Ghassanah. They are indifferent to the jokes about this boasting told by other families.

After the Bank was occupied in 1967, people started making predictions, some pessimistic, some optimistic, about when the Israelis would withdraw. Someone said, "I'm sure Israel will withdraw after a year."

His friend, who was from the Husseini family, responded, "What rot! How can Israel withdraw from the Bank after a year? The Barghoutis have been here for five hundred years and they still haven't withdrawn!"

Ironically, no sooner has Anis finished speaking than he stops the car and turns off the engine in obedience to an order from an Israeli woman soldier and her male companion, who clearly are guarding the main gateway to the settlement.

"Where are you going?" asks the female soldier in American English.

"To Deir Ghassanah," answers Anis.

"Get out of the car, please."

"Excuse me?"

"Get out of the car."

Anis gets out.

"License."

Tamim understands that Uncle Anis is in some kind of difficulty and wants to find out what, so he opens the car door and asks, with an innocence incomprehensible in Halamish, "What's up, Uncle Anis?" Immediately he finds the female soldier's machine gun aimed at him. "Stay where you are! Close the door!" she yells in his face.

I think it's very odd for them to ask for his driver's license and wonder if her English isn't that good and she meant to say 'ID card.'

Anis, even more taken aback than I, asks her, also in American English, "Which license?"

"Your license and the registration."

Anis hands her the registration and starts searching for his driver's license in his small wallet, where he doesn't find it, and then in his pockets, where he doesn't find it either.

The tension on the female soldier's face is plain. She orders us all out of the car and the male soldier immediately joins her, his finger on the trigger of his rifle. He talks with his comrade in Hebrew, asking what the problem is. She tells him and backs away a little so he can get closer.

"You are in violation of the law and under arrest. We shall take you to Bet-El for interrogation and you will be punished. Understood?"

"I'm the undersecretary of the Ministry of Planning in the Palestinian Authority. This is my identity card."

Anis takes out his ID and the male soldier takes and keeps it.

Anis goes on: "I left the license at home by mistake. I live here in Deir Ghassanah, so I can bring it to you in ten minutes."

The male soldier exchanges some words in Hebrew with his female companion.

"You are in violation of the law."

"What's the driver's license got to do with you? Are you a traffic policeman? Only the Palestinian traffic police can punish me, which it will have the right to do. This is what the agreement between us says."

"I don't know anything about agreements. Screw agreements. Here the only law is the law of the State of Israel, understand?"

It appears Anis has thought of another way out and tries it, on the off chance. He starts going through the papers in his wallet. Then he pulls something out.

"Also I have U.S. nationality. I'm a U.S. citizen and this is my U.S. social security number. Do you stop U.S. citizens?"

"You are in violation of Israeli law. I want the license. Don't you understand?"

Then the soldier starts yelling at the top of his voice in a hectoring, didactic tone: "This is the State of Israel, understand? You are driving a car in the State of Israel."

The female conscript raises her gun and the male soldier starts yelling even louder. "You are driving your car in the State of Israel."

His voice rises even higher.

"You have to respect the law of the State of Israel! Understand?"

"We are not in the State of Israel here. Also, I'm an undersecretary and not a child driving without a license. I'll bring you the license in ten minutes and . . . ."

The soldier interrupts.

"It is forbidden to drive a car one meter without a license."

I take a couple of steps forward and ask, "I'm Jordanian and I have a Jordanian license. I'll go, get the license from his house, and come back. Is that possible?"

"You're Jordanian?"

"Yes."

"Give me your passport."

"Here."

"Do you have a driver's license?"

"Yes."

"Go. Go, all of you. He stays here."

I take a step toward Anis and ask him, "Where will I find your license, Anis?"

"In the drawer. In the desk drawer. Or ask Zaghlula."

We set off in the car, leaving our cousin, Assistant Undersecretary at the Ministry of Planning and International Assistance in the Palestinian National Authority, hostage to the soldiers of the settlement of Halamish.

I drive fast from Halamish to Beit Rima and then to Deir Ghassanah.

We stop in front of Anis's house, the first in the village.

Husam and I get out. Quickly we go inside.

Zaghlula appears in the courtyard, a troubled expression furrowing her face when she notices that I'm driving her brother's car and he's not with us.

"Don't worry. We need Anis's driver's license."

"And where's Anis?"

"At Halamish."

She climbs with me the staircase leading to Anis's room. We search in the drawers and every other possible place. We don't find the license. We go back to the car.

"Who's with you in the car?"

"Tamim and Ya'qoub."

Her emotions are torn between welcoming Tamim and anxiety over her brother.

"Welcome, welcome!"

"We have to go back to Anis. Excuse us."

I drive back in the direction of Halamish, afraid that they may have taken him off to Bet-El and made things even more complicated. I intend to try to persuade them to let him go with me and get the license himself but I'm not optimistic. Husam, mixing seriousness and humor, says, "Your cousin Anis is an admirer of the Oslo Agreement and of all agreements signed, not signed, and to be signed. He admires the peace and Palestinian moderation and moderates, and this is the result. He's been made to eat shit. Serves him right."

Close to Beit Rima, we're surprised to find Anis walking alone, returning to Deir Ghassanah. They've let him go without waiting for us to come back with the license.

Anis gets in and explodes. "The bastards just wanted to have a bit of fun with us. Two guards fed up with being on duty at the settlement gate, so they decide to use us for entertainment. The moment you left with the car, they gave me back my papers and told me bye-bye. I asked, 'What about the license?' They said they didn't need it."

Then he remembers that our whole trip is for Tamim.

"I'm sorry, Tamim. I wish you could have entered the village in a nicer way. What have they got to do with driver's licenses? And I don't know what made me forget my license on this of all days. Damn it!"

This is how Tamim entered Deir Ghassanah for the first time in his life: checkpoint—pointed machine guns—driver's license—Bet-El— "This is the State of Israel!"—"Understand?"—"Respect the law of the state!" And the first Barghouti he saw in the village he didn't have time to shake hands with or hug.

I say to myself, he'll go through what I did the day I first returned two years ago. His fingers will gradually exchange the touch of velvet for that of cactus—the mountain top of the imagined for the valley of the actual.

In our dreams we draw them as rainbows, but homelands aren't our poems of homelands, and when they are afflicted with occupation, poverty, and a costly endurance, the gray halo to their rainbow becomes thicker than anyone could imagine. Then I catch myself and think again: Tamim's response may be different from mine in the end. I come burdened with my past. He starts from the white page of the future. I think, this page is his; it's his to color as he chooses and to narrate as and when he wishes.

To make Anis feel better, Tamim says, "The important thing is that you're okay, Uncle Anis. We're the ones who should apologize for all this trouble we've put you to."

For Tamim, Deir Ghassanah is, before any other house, the Ra'd House, 'Dar Ra'd,' and before any other face, the face of my uncle's wife, the ample Umm Talal. On our arrival, Umm Talal rushes out beaming, hugs him, and lets out a trill of joy to celebrate his arrival.

The neighbors of Dar Ra'd gather to greet us or rather, this time, to greet Tamim. I say 'greet' and not 'get to know.' I'm sure they 'know' him already—know what he looks like: athletic, on the tall side, his eyes black, his hair black and strong as a horse's. What other topic of conversation is there in the houses of Deir Ghassanah than the news of their sons and grandsons, off in faraway countries?

The absent are the talk of their evening gatherings on winter nights around the stoves and pots of tea. They are the objects of their anxiety whenever the weather, or political, conditions in their countries of exile turn nasty. The village knows their names down to the youngest grandchild and knows their characters and what they look like. It knows who was born, who got married, who fell ill, who was given a ten-dinar pay raise, and who quarreled with his wife or his mother-in-law or his director at work. It knows who got rich and who went bankrupt, who was taken into detention, who obtained his family reunification papers, who did well at school, and who failed. And all this without meeting any of them.

Tamim asks, "Where's the room? Where were you born, Baba?"

We enter the large room with the high dome and the four piers that meet in the middle, from which an electric bulb now dangles in place of the oil lamp of 1944.

"I was born here, Tamim."

The word 'here' takes me to everything that is 'there.' It takes me to the houses of exile. It takes me to times that overlap in my mind. It flies with me from 'my' room here and Tamim's silence to searching in 1963 for a place to rent in the Agouza district of Cairo, to asking for the timetable for the first days of studies at the university there, to driving over the Margaret bridge between Buda and Pest in Hungary, to sleeping on the floor in the Khalifa Prison in Cairo, to the soldier kicking me with his boot in my right kidney to wake me up so that I could be expelled from Cairo at dawn when Tamim was a five-month-old child, and to Radwa's voice as she curses the officers and then cries after they leave, taking me with them for an absence that will last seventeen years. The word 'here' flies me to a apartment in the Mkahhal Building in the Fakihani district of Beirut, the studios of the Voice of Palestine in the building opposite, and to the rooms of hotels, too numerous to count, where I and other young men argue with delegations and organizations from around the world over a comma or half a sentence in order to assert our right to self-determination and in defense of the PLO. I see the PLO's leadership bending its backbone lower, year after year, under every successive pressure until it has lost its posture altogether, while I raise objections and protest in prose, in poetry, and by keeping my distance. Paradoxically, the political mistakes of the PLO then brought me back to 'here' under a nonsensical selectivity that permitted my return but not that of my brothers or their children—Ghassan, Ghada, Ghadeer, Fadi, Shadi, Yara, Lara, Sara, Dima, Dara, and Muhammad. How did politics come to play this back-to-front game with us? Is it enough that by pure coincidence I met the conditions that determined the numbers of Palestinians Israel would allow to return? Is it enough that as an observer at the Palestinian National Council I should be allowed to return?

What kind of a paradox is this?

Does the blind dog of politics wag its tail in greeting to an enemy like me?

And I'm an opponent both calm and rude. I have got out and continue to get out my message of opposition and I shall go on doing so in the future too despite my 'benefiting' from the policy that I criticize even when I'm here.

Later, six years after this incident, on the stage of the Palace of Culture in Ramallah and at an occasion entirely conducive to praise and gratitude (my reception of the Palestine Award for Poetry), I will stand up to thank the prize committee for choosing me and criticize the leadership, the Authority, and the government, in the presence of the leadership, who are sitting in the front rows of the spacious hall, and in front of a thousand people who have come to attend the celebration. I will call for the correction of mistakes "even at the top of the page," the "top of the page" being the prime minister seated in the front row alongside most of the Authority's leading men.

I was born here, Tamim.

I move on with him into the next room, which now belongs to Umm Talal, my uncle's wife, and from there to the one beyond it.

"Here in this room, three-quarters of a century or more ago, stood your great-grandfather, entirely alone, with his stick carved from an oak tree, his white kufiya, his goat's-hair head rope, and his long brown mantle, dancing with the reflection of his shadow on this wall opposite the oil lamp because he was so delighted at having obtained the agreement of your grandmother, Umm 'Ata, to the engagement of his son 'Abd al-Razeq to her daughter Sakina—the very beautiful, very intelligent girl with the green eyes and smooth chestnut hair who was the cleverest girl in the school and the prettiest in the village. An old man alone in a large gothic room with a dome, piers, and walls so white the plaster shone, dancing with his own shadow, bending right and bending left and shaking his stick ecstatically in the air in each direction, no music accompanying his dance but the silence of the night and the hissing of the lamp, no companions about him to share his wondrous celebration but the beating of his heart and the surges of a joy that couldn't wait for the morning's sun."

Tamim was clearly bemused.

"Who told you that story, Dad?"

"Your aunt, Umm al-Nahed. She said she went to see him at Dar Ra'd and found him dancing with his shadow and waving his stick in the air without uttering a word. She joined in with him without knowing what the occasion was. She didn't ask him and he didn't open his mouth. He kept on dancing and she left him at it."

We leave the room and go out into the courtyard garden once more.

Tamim wants to see where the huge fig tree had stood, the one that was cut down by my uncle's wife because she couldn't find anyone to eat its fruit any more, and the different rooms of the Ra'd house—my uncle 'Ata's, my uncle Abu Muti''s, and Abu Hussein's—along with the mosque, the square, the village guesthouse, the school, and 'Ein al-Deir spring, and to make a tour of the whole village. Tamim says nothing but his eyes never stop talking and I hear his eyes well, this being the job of fathers and mothers. I wish that by a miracle he could see all four seasons at Deir Ghassanah at the same instant, see the huge almond trees—first sun-dappled, then bare, then wet, then covered in fruit—at the same time. I want the birds to come all together in all their kinds, with their names, their colors, their silences, and their beaks, so that he can see them as a single flock. I want al-Sa'id Dhib's mare to pass us now, neighing and striking the Ruweis road with her hooves before his ears and eyes. Tamim wants his imagination to be translated into stones. I want the stones to put strength back into my middle-aged imagination that has stuck with me all my life. This is not the time to think about the mystery behind the disappointment that comes with every return and how knowledge of the past spoils the present that is before one's eyes. Tamim's past in Deir Ghassanah has yet to be formed. He has no disappointments and nothing has spoiled his expectations yet. Disappointment afflicts those who would like to recover their past, not those who have no past. I say to myself, let me then be silent and let him see.

After the drinks in the courtyard that hospitality requires, we excuse ourselves to Umm Talal and leave, with a promise to return later for lunch.

Tamim says, "I'll be able to tell the places on my own. I'm going to walk in front of you."

No one gets lost in Deir Ghassanah. I tell him to try.

He steps over the high lintel of the gate to Dar Ra'd. Before us are the hills, the Ruweis and Sahayil fields, the road to 'Ein al-Deir, and a fence of cactus, its spiny paddles in a row overlooking the road that runs around the village. We turn left into the lane that leads to the village square.

He points to his right and says, "That's Dar Salih."

He crosses the square to its far end and stands on the built-in bench.

"This is the village guesthouse."

We pass the village guesthouse and go to the guesthouse of Shaykh Matar, say hello to the people there, and resume the tour at a leisurely pace.

After a while, a very thin person whom I don't know greets us. Husam speaks to him for a little and then tells him jokingly, "Tell Abu Tamim what happened to you at the Hebrew University. Tell him why they threw you out of your job. This is the son of . . ."— he mentions a name. "Do you remember him?"

Husam's question embarrasses me as I don't recognize the man and don't hear clearly the name that Husam mentions. I ask him, "What happened?"

"Before the Intifada, a long time ago, they gave me a job at the Hebrew University in Jerusalem."

"As a teacher at the university?" I ask him.

"Heavens no! Me? A teacher? I can't read or write."

"What job did they give you at the university?"

"Monkey keeper."

"Monkey keeper?"

"Monkey keeper in the labs, the university labs. Experimental monkeys. They call them 'experimental monkeys,' cousin."

"How many monkeys?"

"Six or seven."

"And what were your tasks?"

"I was supposed to feed the monkeys at set times. They gave me tins of milk so I said to myself, now you're in clover. I drank the milk, of course. I'd drink three quarters of it or more and give a sip or two to each monkey and no one had any idea what was going on. There wasn't a single tin of milk in our entire village."

"And they found out, of course."

"They saw that I was getting healthier and the monkeys were close to dying of hunger. They threw me out. Those were good times, I swear."

"And then what?"

"Then there was the Intifada and you couldn't find work for love or money, God help us."

I look around me for Tamim and find him holding Abu Hasan by the hand.

Abu Hasan is ninety years old, or a little less, and can hardly see, though with his clean double-breasted robe, white head cloth, and rope retainer tipped a little to one side he looks younger.

Tamim says that the moment the man sensed he was close to him he seized his hand.

"Take me to the mosque, son."

Tamim says to me, "I didn't know what to tell him. How could I explain to him that I'd only set foot in the village two hours ago and I didn't know where anything was? I was too embarrassed to explain so I took his hand and said to him, 'This way, please.'"

"Hasan won't be coming this week. He won't be taking me to the mosque. You take me to the mosque."

"After two or three steps, he almost tripped over a stone in a narrow alleyway between the houses. When I told him to take care, he started telling me the story of the alleyway and how he was the one who'd drawn a line there with his hoe to stop the late Abu Yusuf from encroaching on the property of the late Abu Zuheir. 'I stuck my hoe in the ground and said, "This is where you stop."' He paused and suddenly looked at me suspiciously. I could see him squinting like someone who wants to be sure of who it is he's seeing. Then he asked me, 'Who are you?'"

'I'm Tamim.'

'Tamim son of who?'

'Son of Mourid.'

'Mourid son of who?'

'Son of 'Abd al-Razeq.'

"Abd al-Razeq son of who?"

'Son of Muhammad al-Turrad.'

'Ah. I know him. He was my friend. Your grandfather's grandfather was my friend, son. And he was a poet. The whole village knew him. All the villages around knew him. He wasn't your grandfather's grandfather, he was your grandfather's father. God rest his soul and those of all our dead.'

'Amen.'

. . .

'Do you know any of his poems by heart?'

"He gave a long sigh, closed his eyes, and recited:

'*This stick of mine's from a tree.*
It helps me see.
It'll still be there,
When I'm no longer here.'

"He recited from memory, with mistakes in the meter of course, but he was proud he still remembered his old friend's poetry."

Husam has moved a little distance from us but now rejoins us and he tells us the never-to-be-forgotten tale of Abu Hasan and Abu Yusuf.

Abu Yusuf's house was huge and had two stories and he was very proud of how much taller his house was than all the other houses of Deir Ghassanah. Abu Hasan was a young man. Like everyone else in the village, he had to sit and listen to the pride and boasting but could think of nothing to say back, until poverty drove him to make the journey to Beirut, where he worked as porter at the harbor and from which he returned with some money and some 'knowledge of the world.' He declared, "Abu Yusuf boasts he can look down on the whole village from his second story. I swear to God, people, in Beirut I saw a dog looking down from the tenth story!"

We go to the village school. Schools stay in their places; we're the ones who leave. I left the childhood that I spent here half a century ago and turned my face toward Tamim's. The years passed for both of us and at this instant our two childhoods meet at the door of the first school under this first sky.

In the long lane, lined on either side with cypress trees of amazing height, and then at the threshold to the school and among its arches, I think of Tamim's childhood, spent in Cairo and Budapest, and of mine, spent here in Deir Ghassanah. The distance between them is the distance between two planets.

From the moment he was born, he found in front of him everything he needed, everything appropriate to his age, everything that would keep him happy. When he grew older, he found a computer in front of him. He took thirty lessons in piano with Prof. Kati Forrai in Budapest. He couldn't take the discipline at five but later moved on to study in Cairo the oriental oud, which he learned to play expertly. This helped him to pick up quickly the music of ancient Arabic poetry with its sixteen meters and he learned to write the classical Arabic verse forms and to appreciate the Arabic classics, such as the Suspended Odes and the verses of al-Mutanabbi and Abu Tammam. In Budapest, he fell in love with Lego and all the different things you can make with it, and one day he kept asking for a Lego castle with flags flapping on its battlements. We couldn't find one in Budapest, so we brought it for him from Vienna. It was the castle he had in mind but there weren't any flags in the box, so we bought him a small game that included flags and used these for his historic castle. The blessing of exile (and exile has its blessings, which cannot be denied) gave him visits to museums, films and plays to watch, experience of live music. He acquired whatever musical instruments he wanted and at one time had a harmonica, a guitar, a violin, and an oud. It was lucky he didn't fall in love with the piano or we would have had to go without supper.

Our teacher, 'Abd al-Mu'ti, took my earlobe between his fingers and pressed. It hurt a little. He pressed more and it hurt more. The children in the classroom laughed at what was happening to me so I cried. I cried because I was young (not yet six), because he was punishing me in front of the whole class, and because, like anyone subjected to punishment, I felt I'd done nothing to deserve it. It was all because my mother had decided one day to take me to 'Abd al-Mu'ti's house, where I heard her telling him, "So you want to deprive him of schooling just because of three or four months, Abu Marwan? Shame on you! You did harm enough to me when you stopped me from finishing my own education."

"Me, Umm Mounif? I took your side and your mother knows I did my best. God forgive them, they were stronger than all of us."

"May God not forgive them, in this world or the next! Let's stick to the boy."

"Umm Mounif, your son isn't of school age yet. The laws . . . ."

She interrupts him in exasperation.

"What laws? And who made the laws?"

"He has to be fully six years old to be admitted to the school."

"He'll be six in two or three months."

"It's just not possible, and it's in his interest, so he can take in the lessons and not fail the first year and get a complex."

"The boy's clever, Abu Marwan. Cleverer than all the boys from the village that you've accepted. I know every one of them. Mourid is the cleverest of them all, as you'll find out. Also, he has his brother Mounif's books and he's always got a pen in his hand at home. He can write the alphabet now, his handwriting's good, and he's memorized lots of songs. If you gave him the exam today he might pass."

"Umm Mounif, they check and send inspectors and it would be embarrassing for me. If one of the inspectors discovered that he was too young . . . ."

"And why should the inspector find out he's too young?"

"He'll find out, and the school administration will be blamed because of me and . . . ."

She interrupts him again.

"Accept him, Abu Marwan, and when the inspector comes, send him out of the classroom. He stays out for one period and no harm done. Or make him get under his desk and hide, he's small enough anyway . . . ."

"He wasn't small a minute ago, Umm Mounif!"

He laughed and added, "All right, Umm Mounif. He'll start school, for your sake, but when the inspector comes he has to hide or get out. I'll persuade the headmaster."

My mother thanked him and next morning told Mounif, "Take your brother with you today, dear, and leave him in Class One. I've spoken to Abu Marwan and he says yes."

We went back to the house. We found that my father had got back from work and she told him she'd succeeded in getting me into school. My father was embarrassed and hated the idea of having asked his cousin Abu Marwan for a personal favor, but my mother wouldn't be put off and refused to let me lose a whole year because of a law she thought was stupid.

That evening, she took the scissors and a piece of thick linen cloth, made me a bag, which she would always refer to as a 'case,' and put in it a pencil and a new exercise book on which she had handwritten 'Mourid 'Abd al-Razeq al-Barghouti, Class One, Deir Ghassanah Boys School.'

(A long parenthesis. Later, I will discover that my name in my birth certificate isn't Mourid at all. How I found this out is a story that bided its time until I reached Third Year Preparatory, or Class Nine, at Ramallah Boys Secondary. The Ministry of Education had decided to introduce a Preparatory Certificate. The headmaster asked us to

I WAS BORN THERE, I WAS BORN HERE

provide the entry requirements for the certificate exam, which were ten Jordanian dinars and an original birth certificate. I went home, asked my parents for my birth certificate, and was confronted with one in the name of Nawaf 'Abd al-Razeq al-Barghouti. In amazement I yelled, "This isn't my birth certificate!" Things became clear when they told me that when I was born, my parents had decided to call me Mourid. After two or three days, they sent the midwife to the headman of Deir Ghassanah to ask him to issue an official birth certificate. The midwife, Amna al-Warda, went in to see Abu Rasim the headman and told him that 'Abd al-Razeq (otherwise known as Abu Mounif) had been blessed with a male child and she'd been sent to get a stamped birth certificate. He got his papers ready and asked her the child's name. The midwife had forgotten the name, which wasn't common in Deir Ghassanah, or anywhere in the country for that matter. She tried to remember but it was useless, and was the headman going to hold up his business because of the midwife's stupidity? He told her, "You don't have to remember the name. His brother's Mounif, so he'll be Nawaf": at his own whim, the headman chose me a name close to my elder brother's and entered it in my birth certificate. He made his thumb print and stamped it and it was done. When Amna al-Warda returned with the stamped certificate, they stuffed it in with the other papers without checking and no one asked for it until the headmaster, because of the newly introduced exam. All through the nine preceding years, I'd been registered as Mourid al-Barghouti. In any case, once I'd explained things to him the headmaster agreed to let me take the exam under my freshly discovered name of Nawaf, as in the original certificate, and that is what happened. From then on, all my official papers have been in the name of Nawaf and no one outside the family and a small number of close friends knows this name, none of whom ever calls me by it. I refused to acknowledge, as did my family, my made-up name. We behaved as though it didn't exist. I went on being known everywhere as Mourid and I publish my books, articles, and poems under the name Mourid al-Barghouti, a name that I love as much as I hate my official name.)

Mounif, who is three years older than I, was in Class Four, and he took me with him, the linen 'case'—containing my exercise book and one pencil—in my hand. No sooner had we separated in the school corridor and I'd entered the classroom than silent tears flowed down my cheeks. I sat down in the last seat. I felt afraid of all the children. I felt as though I was in the village guesthouse in the middle of all the grown-ups, not in the Class One classroom. When the teacher came in for the first period, I went up to him, crying, and told him, "Take me to Class Four, Sir."

"Where?"

"To my big brother."

"To whom?"

"To my brother Mounif."

"Go and sit down in your seat."

I went, still crying. The teacher left and came back with Mounif. The moment I saw him I forgot my tears and felt happy. Mounif hugged me, wiped away the tears with his fingers, and sat down close by my side.

"I want to stay with you. I don't like this school."

"Don't be afraid. Don't be afraid. We'll go home together after the last bell."

That is how I became a pupil in Class One at the Deir Ghassanah school.

The terrifying inspector came, of course. I ducked my head and disappeared beneath the desk, as agreed. Toward the end of the year, the inspector came again and again I dived straight under the desk and held my breath. The plan would have succeeded if the inspector hadn't asked the children a question—I don't remember exactly what now.

Not one child raised his finger to answer and when he called on one of them to do so, he answered wrongly. I was almost dying of fury because I knew the answer but was forbidden to appear. Suddenly, I popped up from my hiding place, stretched myself to my full height, raised my hand as far as it would go, and cried out, "Me, sir! Me, sir!"

Mr. 'Abd al-Mu'ti was speechless.

The inspector heard my answer and said, "Bravo, my boy. Correct. But why were you underneath the desk?"

I looked at him and then at Mr. 'Abd al-Mu'ti standing next to him and said, "Because I'm too young."

The children laughed and even the inspector laughed, but Mr. 'Abd al-Mu'ti didn't laugh. I sat down. As soon as the inspector had gone, the teacher came back alone, called me out, and started rubbing my right ear between his finger and thumb and shaking my head from side to side.

"What have you gone and done?"

"Sorry, sir."

"Go back to your seat. I'll handle it."

He did handle it, though I don't know how things were smoothed over. In any case, I continued, took the exam, and came top of the class. Abu Marwan went to my parents and congratulated my mother and father, saying, "Take good care of him. God protect him."

"When the village stopped me from continuing my education, Abu Marwan, I couldn't take them on. But now the education of my children has become my whole life."

"May God punish those who were behind it. It wasn't just you they wronged, Umm Mounif. They wronged all the girls of the village."

Abu Marwan was the first communist in Deir Ghassanah. He held what in those days were called 'progressive' ideas but was a lone voice crying out in a village of massive locks, confident in its darkness, which could defeat him but which he could not defeat. My mother wasn't ready for marriage because she was still under fourteen. She didn't know who my father was when they mentioned his name in front of her as a possible groom. In fact, her young heart had been bewitched since she was nine by a boy, a relative of hers, who was somewhat older than she. He used to bring her nice gifts of books with colored pictures and drawings and encouraged her to go to school and made her memorize lines from old poetry. She called her attachment to him true love and never forgot it or tired of recalling it, sometimes as a love story, sometimes as a childish crush, and sometimes as a matter of admiration and need; in her lively imagination he remained a beautiful dream that had been shattered. The boy disappeared from her life the moment they engaged her to my father. He left Palestine to continue his education and returned to marry another woman; he died decades ago at an early age. An entire life has passed since these events, and now, at almost ninety, she still remembers how happy he made her childhood, even though she was a poor orphan, and tells us, often with invisible tears in her eyes, her story, down to the most precise details, as though it were happening to her now; in fact, she demands that I write it down.

She says: "It wasn't just me they wronged. They wronged your father too. He didn't know me and had never seen me before in his life. They said, 'So-and-so is for so-and-so' and that was that. It wasn't your father's fault. They wronged us both. Take it as my testament to you all: 'Treat your daughters fairly.' Nobody should impose their will on anybody else when it comes to marriage."

She no longer wants anything from the story but the story itself, especially now that, except for her, none of the actors is still living. I hear her calling down death on those who prevented her from going to school.

"They died long ago, Mother."

To which she replies, "I wish they could die twenty times."

We return from the school and when we reach the square again, some-one comes and tells us that lunch is ready at Umm Talal's.

Marwan al-Barghouti phones and I tell him we're at Deir Ghassanah.

"I'll be there in half an hour."

"You'll find a splendid lunch waiting for you."

Tamim, as it happens, has been dreaming of eating musakhan and his hopes are not disappointed. His grandmother introduced him to musakhan in Amman, though always with the reminder that "musakhan's different in our village" and "real musakhan is the type made in the clay oven," meaning the musakhan of Deir Ghassanah.

We take our seats around the lunch table in the garden. A whole chicken per person on a large loaf of bread coated with olive oil and then roasted, the chicken split open down the middle, basted in oil, roasted, and then covered in sumac, with lots of minced onions fried in olive oil piled on it and on the bread. The bread has been baked on the ruzuf (hot stones the size of large walnuts) of the clay oven, covered with large quantities of fried onions and sumac, placed particularly in the hollows made in the loaf by the stones. Next to this is a bowl of buttermilk and another of finely chopped green salad as well as tahini and chili peppers. A glass of hot tea with mint or sage comes as a necessary finishing touch to an amazing meal of this type.

Anis says to Tamim jokingly, noticing how much pleasure he is taking in the food, "Don't eat too much! You've still got the poetry evening and I'm afraid you'll fall asleep."

We go to the square.

I don't know where the villagers have found all the plastic chairs, which they have set out in rows. Together we climb the steps to the village guesthouse.

I remind the audience of my last encounter with them, two years before in this very square, and say that tonight I am back, bringing my son with me for an evening of two poets. I read them a number of my new poems and then ask their permission to introduce Tamim to them myself.

"This young man, born in Egypt of an Egyptian mother, who has spent all his life away from you and who saw Deir Ghassanah for the first time only three hours ago, will read poems about Palestine, some written in classical Arabic and some in the Palestinian dialect, and he'll sing country songs—the 'ataba, mijana, and dal'ona. If you think it was his Palestinian father who put Palestine in his heart and mind, you should know that it was his Egyptian mother, Radwa Ashour, who made it her business to nurture his Palestinian identity out of her love for Palestine, so allow me to send her a greeting from here and tell her that Tamim is now reading his poetry in the square of Deir Ghassanah."

I wanted to speak of Radwa in the square of Deir Ghassanah and to the people of Deir Ghassanah because it wouldn't be natural if Radwa's almost total knowledge of everything about the village and its people—their names and life stories, the funny things they're known for and their sorrows—were to remain one-sided. I wanted them to know her too. I wanted her to enter their houses without a visa from the State of Israel. Radwa will probably never see Deir Ghassanah with her own eyes nor Deir Ghassanah her. Radwa will never consent to line up in front of the Israeli embassy in Cairo to ask for a visa.

Then I turn to Tamim and tell him, "If you want to be a poet, you have to begin here, among your own people and on this land."

As he begins reading, astonishment shows on their faces at his village dialect that is no different from theirs. After reading them his poems, he sings them verses in the 'ataba and mijana forms:

My country, forgive us if we've sinned.
We set off to come to you but to others inclined.
Stitch us in with the threads of your robe's design.
Shame it were, that we be strangers in your land.

Anyone with a stick waved it in the air. Any woman good at trilling the ululations of celebration did so for this boy come from a country she didn't know. The girls clapped for a long time and whispered among themselves. Handsome young 'Abd al-Latif al-Barghouti climbed from the audience to Tamim's side and started reciting more 'ataba and mijana, in turn with him. At this (extremely rare) literary celebration of theirs, the people of the village almost forgot that basically they were weary, very weary, in a village sunk in weariness.

Later, nine whole years after we stood there, Tamim and his poetry will take on a different meaning for the people of Deir Ghassanah. They and the people of the surrounding villages will come to hear his verses. The people will fill the school playground. The child born in the Dr. Gohar Maternity Hospital on the banks of the Nile in Cairo will become the young poet of Palestine and its handsome son, with his long flowing verses, his smile, and the message of hope that these brought them, despite the long-lasting national dejection. This was a new son who was 'theirs.' This was a son they had discovered unexpectedly as they went about their normal daily acts of resistance and endurance. He had arrived 'ready-made,' as though he'd been born standing like that in some distant place and had come back to them.

Your Palestinian message, Radwa, had arrived.

5

The Identity Card

Each of our relatives and friends wants to invite us to lunch or dinner, or offers to go with us in the car to show us the village, or for a walk in the streets of Ramallah and al-Bireh. We prefer walks so that Tamim can see as much as possible of the houses, gardens, trees, and humans. On two separate occasions, I see the Namiq and avoid him, as usual.

By coincidence, when turning the key in the door of the apartment, I discover that a friend is living in the apartment next to ours in the Yasmin Building. He says his wife is working outside the country now and he's living alone but will cook us an Italian dinner. He also surprises me by telling me that another friend of ours is living in the building. I go to see this other friend, leaving Tamim to rest a little.

We speak about many things. Then I say to him, "Lots of people have asked me why you accepted the position of minister, and I couldn't defend your decision."

"Of course. You never will be able to defend it. It was indefensible."

"So why did you do it, when ministers used to tremble at the mere mention of your name in the days you were an MP investigating their corrupt practices?"

"No one really wants to uncover the corruption and I was getting nowhere. They offered me the job so I took it."

"And where did all the effort you'd put in go?"

"Nowhere."

"Do you know someone called Namiq?"

"Namiq al-Tijani?"

"Yes."

"Did he cheat you?"

"He cheated all of you."

"I know that."

"No punishment?"

"From time to time they punish people like that by reducing their rewards. Then they give them many times more."

"They've asked me to supervise a cultural project of which he's one of the main employees. The project's faltering and it seems they want to save what can be saved. They said they were looking for someone who could be trusted with the money, someone to curb the expenditures and speed up the work so as to finish the project."

"Did you agree?"

"I asked for time to think."

"When do they want you?"

"Next year, in March."

"Did they offer you a guarantee that they wouldn't interfere in your areas of responsibility?"

"We haven't got into details yet."

"They'll give you the guarantee."

"Good."

"But at the first clash, they'll abandon you, all of them."

"So?"

"Accept."

"Why should I accept?"

"To save what can be saved, my friend!"

I leave my friend and return to the apartment to go with Tamim to Ziryab's café to show him Taysir's drawings. I find him in the doorway on his way out. He opens his arms to hug me and yells, "Uncle Abu Saji called!"

I hug him and push him back into the apartment.

"What are you waiting for? Call a taxi straightaway."

We go to the office and Abu Saji stands, holding up Tamim's identity card in his right hand.

He hugs him and gives him the card.

He calls a number on his cell phone and hands the phone to Tamim: "Speak to Dr. Ashour."

My mind is wandering so much I don't hear what Tamim says to Radwa. I see him hugging the violin, gazing at it and touching it gently, his face full of light and triumph. He was less than two years old and had left our table at the Restaurant Budapest, gone over on his own to the gypsy band, and stood in front of the wooden stage, watching the violins and the players with interest. They were playing the pisirta, their most famous and popular piece, which depicts a flock of birds circling in fluent coordination. At first, the violins seem more delicate than the smile of a sleeping baby; then the playing suddenly increases in tension: a wind has arisen, carrying one of the birds far from its companions. In a crescendo, the feverish music rages, depicting the flock searching for its missing member, or the bird searching for the flock. Then we hear the bird's song, approaching gradually from the distance until it fills the foreground. All the players have stopped now except for the soloist, whose violin is transformed into a singing bird (this is considered a display of supreme mastery and skill). Finally, the violins return, playing their concluding tune, celebrating the return of the bird and the completion of the encounter with a joyous, festive melody to the enthusiastic applause of the revelers. Tamim kept clapping along with the rest and Radwa and I watched him without interfering, as he wasn't annoying anyone. Suddenly, the principal player went forward to Tamim, smiling, held out his violin, and left it in his safekeeping. Tamim kept gazing at the violin, touching it and then gazing at it again until the next set began and the player took back his instrument with a kind smile. We got up and thanked him and Tamim came back with us to the table.

For a long while after that night, the Budapest was the only restaurant he would let us go to. Eventually, though, Tamim worked out for himself that most restaurants in the city, and the whole of Hungary, serve their dinners to the accompaniment of similar gypsy bands. The two weeks when he was with me during his half-term vacation and the three months of the summer holiday each year were festivals that he would dream about throughout the months he was at school in Cairo.

Later, after thirteen years of residence in Budapest and after my return to Cairo, I will come to realize, from Radwa and from Tamim, as well as from what I deduce without either saying anything, that Radwa has had to put up not only with my absence and the burdens of raising Tamim, as a baby, a child, and an only boy, and protecting him from harm, she has also had to put up with his insistence on going to Budapest. Budapest was associated in his mind with our being together as a family and with the holidays and fun and a sense of security and freedom. Cairo, on the other hand, was associated with homework and discipline and getting up early and exams. Not to mention that Cairo had expelled his father.

The worst moments for Tamim were when he boarded the Malev plane at Budapest Airport on his way back to Cairo. They were so bad that once he said to his mother and me as we were on our way there, "I hope the plane crashes." The most beautiful moments in his life were when he boarded the Malev plane at Cairo Airport to go to Budapest.

His school holidays began before those of the university where Radwa works and he refused to wait until they could travel together to Budapest. Instead he'd insist on going to me on his own, immediately, while Radwa had to wait for her holidays to begin and then catch up with him. He was less than five years old when he boarded the plane on his own for the first time. She had arranged for the airline to take care of him on the plane and to hand him over to me at Budapest Airport, and at the airport they allowed me to wait for him at the foot of the steps leading down from the plane. No sooner did the plane open its doors than I saw him, flanked by two flight attendants, one holding his right hand, the other his left, a red tape across the stairway in front of them. I went up the steps at a run. They removed the tape and the way he hugged me made it unnecessary for them to demand proof that he was mine. One of the flight attendants told me as I thanked them, "He's a wonderful boy. He speaks Hungarian like a Hungarian. God protect him."

The first thing he did was to take off an elegant necklace that hung down to his chest, carrying a card with his and my names on it, my address and my telephone numbers at home and at work.

I told him that I'd been on a plane for the first time when I went to university at the age of nineteen. Then I asked him, "Who hung this card on your chest?"

"The flight attendant told me, 'This is your identity. It has to stay hung on your chest till you meet up with your father.'"

In Abu Saji's office in the Muqata'a, I take the identity card from him, look at it, and hand it back to him.

We thank Abu Saji for getting it done in time to prevent Tamim from being late for university.

We go to a special office where we obtain a permit for departure via the bridge. This departure permit, required for travel to any place outside Palestine, complements the identity card, and has to be shown to the Israeli officer at the bridge.

Tamim's papers are complete. We can leave any time we want. He won't be away from his university for long.

Now that he has his identity card in his hand, I ask him, "When do you want to go back to Cairo?"

"Can we stay here a few days?"

"What about university?"

. . .

"I propose that we go back to Amman tomorrow morning, spend two days with your grandmother Umm Mounif, and then go back to Cairo."

"Okay. But not tomorrow. The day after."

"What do you want to do?"

"Anything."

"Uncle Hikmat wants us to go with him to his house in Jenin."

"Great. I'll see a new city."

"Then we're agreed."

Next day we go to Jenin. We spend a whole day there. It's my first visit too. The conversation revolves around the building of the American University in Jenin and the replanning of the city, and everyone is reassured by the return of normal life to the city. It astonishes me that Jenin is able to offer medical services to our people who remained in their country in 1948 and became Israeli citizens and that Jews also come from there in search of cheaper treatment, especially in dentistry. As a result, Jenin has brought together a large concentration of Palestinian dentists and with each new closure that prevents people from crossing the Green Line they lose money. This was in the years of the high hopes that followed immediately on the Oslo Agreement. The checkpoints, closures, invasions, hunger, detentions, and massacres

will come later. The hopes, dreams, relief, convenience of life, education, commerce, and promise of independence will all be destroyed, at first by degrees and then at one go.

Years later, in 2002, the Israeli army will storm the city of Jenin, impose a siege on its refugee camp, and prevent any type of media and any ambulances from getting close. The people of the camp will show great courage in defending it with the few resources they have and the army will manage to enter only after pulling it down over the heads of its inhabitants, house by house, using tanks and bulldozers and withdrawing only after the massacre is over.

We have been subjected to massacres at intervals throughout our lives. Thus we find ourselves competing in a race between quickly realized mass death and the ordinary life that we dream of every day. One day, I will write a poem called "It's Also Fine":

It's also fine to die in our beds
on a clean pillow
and among our friends.
It's fine to die, once,
our hands crossed on our chests
empty and pale
with no scratches, no chains, no banners,
and no petitions.
It's fine to have an undusty death,
no holes in our shirts,
and no evidence in our ribs.
It's fine to die
with a white pillow, not the pavement, under our cheeks,
our hands resting in those of our loved ones,
surrounded by desperate doctors and nurses,
with nothing left but a graceful farewell,

paying no attention to history,
leaving this world as it is,
hoping that, someday, someone else
will change it.

We return from Jenin before dinner to meet with Marwan al-Barghouti, who tells us he wants to register for a PhD at the College of Economics and Political Sciences at Cairo University and asks Tamim about the requirements for admission and the faculty from whom he might choose a supervisor. We agree that he'll visit us in Cairo and that Tamim will follow up on it once Marwan has decided on the timing.

Marwan does indeed visit us in Cairo, where Radwa and Tamim receive him, and we do in fact begin the admission process for the doctoral program.

When Marwan returns, Ariel Sharon will be preparing to throw out Ehud Barak and quietly taking the first steps to that end.

One year later, Sharon will take one thousand Israeli soldiers with him on a visit that both he and Barak know is a provocation but on which he insists. The general, set on making the leap to leader of the government, will stroll conceitedly, protected by all those soldiers, through the courtyard of the Dome of the Rock and the al-Aqsa Mosque as a way of asserting that it is part of the 'Land of Israel.' He knows very well what he's doing. The general wants a collision; when the collision leads to bloodshed, Sharon will be the solution for the Israelis. They will call on him to lead them.

Sharon got exactly what he wanted. The Palestinians' response would escalate until it culminated in what would later be called 'the Second Intifada.'

The Israeli bull had been let loose in the china shop.

6

The Ambulance

S o this is the Qalandya crossing.

It's changed a lot. It now looks like a terrifying border post between two countries at war, though in fact it's located between Ramallah and Jerusalem, that is, between two cities in Palestine connected by the natural urban growth that fills the sixteen kilometers separating them.

For three or four years after the Oslo Agreement, this Israeli checkpoint between the two cities was one of hundreds of routine checkpoints to be found at the entrances to cities and villages. Later, though, it gradually transformed itself into a permanent and closely guarded border post, intended to prevent any of us from reaching Jerusalem.

There's no need to describe the exceptional tragedies that take place here. The mere likelihood of such things occurring is enough to make the scene appalling. It's enough to picture in one's mind the density and solidity of the fortifications, their iron-ness and cement-ness, and then to picture the fragility of the human body, any human body. It's enough to imagine how a person feels when crammed here for hours waiting for soldiers behind fortified positions to shout through loudspeakers their instructions to stop or to move on through the revolving electronic gates with narrow bars that the Palestinians call 'the milking stalls'—an apt name; in the Hungarian countryside I have seen better set-ups for managing herds of cows.

Here identity cards and permits are checked, at the slowest possible pace. Here bodies, clothes, shoes, bags, feelings, intentions, and expressions are inspected. Here police dogs grant permission to pass or bark in one's face with the zeal on which promotions up the ladder of canine rank perhaps depend. Here are cement blocks, bars, soldiers of numerous facial types (Russians, Falasha from Ethiopia, Poles, Americans from Brooklyn, Arab and oriental Jews), tanks, armored cars, earth-movers, troop carriers, and, all day long, wary faces. A fortress has been improvised here. Hundreds of cars disgorge their passengers, who then stand in rows in the open in all weathers, after which they are permitted to pass, on foot and pulling their bags or carrying them on their heads or backs, among the tanks and machine guns, which are aimed and ready to fire if anything unexpected happens. That's on normal days, so you can imagine how it is today. Arafat's headquarters in Ramallah has been three quarters destroyed and the tanks that surround it day and night are amusing themselves selecting angles at which to bombard the walls, windows, and entrances. They also prevent food and water from reaching the president and his companions and cadres who are trapped with him along with a large number of international supporters from almost all European countries and the U.S.; these include Jews who are critical of the savagery of the Israeli Occupation and who support Palestinian rights. The refugee camps are being invaded. The detainees are in the thousands. It isn't just the Muqata'a or just Arafat; the whole country is under siege. The roads between the cities and the villages are blocked.

The surprising suggestion came from my friend Faisal when he learned that I wanted to get into Ramallah.

"Will you make the journey with me in an ambulance?"

"How?"

"Leave the arrangements to me. I'll phone you tonight to confirm."
We travel together from Amman to the bridge. The travelers are few. We go through the Jordanian police post, then the Israeli police post, and continue to Jericho. There, instead of going to the bus park at the resthouse, we make our way to the hospital, where an ambulance is waiting to take us to Ramallah via the main highway and through the Qalandya checkpoint without our having to get out. It isn't guaranteed since sometimes they search ambulances too but we've decided to risk it. We wait a while for the preparations for departure to be completed. Then it's time. The first time I rode in an ambulance was when I accompanied my brother Mounif. The night rain was heavy over Amman Airport as we stood on the airport runway next to the baggage hold in the belly of the plane from Paris, waiting to receive the coffin. The workers brought it down in the rain, an ordinary wooden coffin bearing numerous seals. I was surprised that the coffin wasn't wrapped in the Palestinian flag. I know that Mounif, though a good citizen, was without official status—neither a king nor a ruler nor a minister nor a top officer—but who ever said that the flag should be used only for those? Mounif had wronged no one in the country, had done no one any harm. He hadn't arrested anyone. He hadn't tortured anyone or been the cause of any of our continual defeats. He was good company, generous, and a man of honor, and flags were created for people like him: they are flown over palaces and in offices in his name, in the name of citizens like him, in the name of us all—ordinary people like you and me and him and her. Is the lot of the good citizen to be a naked wooden coffin such as this on a rainy night such as tonight? If I were ruler, I would give instructions that every citizen who departs this life be covered with the country's flag; that's the least his still living countrymen owe him.

The flag is the flag of the people, of the citizens. The flag is the flag of the ruled, not the ruler.

Many years before, I received a major shock in connection with the flag when the prominent Palestinian historian Emile Touma died before my eyes in the Communist Party Hospital in Budapest. He was suffering from the last stages of cancer and had gone from Nazareth to be treated in Moscow, and from there they sent him Budapest, where he died. Radwa and I visited him daily. George Toubi came from home to accompany the body to Nazareth. Radwa and I bought meters of red, black, green, and white cloth from the market and made a Palestinian flag. We covered the coffin with it and accompanied it to Budapest Airport. At the airport, George stammered a few times before informing us that it would be better to remove the flag from the coffin. Seeing our surprise, he reminded us of something we'd completely forgotten: "They will never let that flag into Ben Gurion Airport. Emile Touma was an Israeli citizen with Israeli nationality. Have you forgotten?"

We had indeed forgotten, Comrade George.

Palestine's great historian and political writer, who, starting at the beginning of the twentieth century, had raised generations in the struggle, was now an Israeli!

We had indeed forgotten, Comrade George.

We removed the Palestinian flag from the historian's coffin.

Mounif comes back from exile with no flag. Emile returns to his homeland with no flag. No flag for the exile, no flag for the resident. We put Mounif in the ambulance and climb in next to him, to accompany him to the Takhassusi Hospital, where he will spend the night alone in the hospital refrigerator, awaiting his final farewell following the next day's noon prayer. I sat next to the coffin, which held within it the secret of his passing, whether natural or by assassination, at the Gare du Nord in the French capital. His mother wasn't with us and couldn't have been. She was waiting for us at the house in al-Shmaysani. Only when she saw us returning from the airport would she believe the fact of his death. She had believed but not believed, still unable to accept that God could do all this to her. Sulafa, Ghassan, Ghada, Ghadeer, Majid, 'Alaa, Talal, and our friend 'Abida had accompanied his body on the way over from Paris. They had had no choice but to believe. They'd believed so much they'd found it in themselves to joke about the ironies of fate.

At a height of thirty-seven thousand feet, my brother Majid asked playfully, "This is the first time we've all traveled together in one plane. Do you think it could go down with all of us on board—Mounif, Sulafa, Ghassan, Ghada, Ghadeer, and me and 'Alaa and Talal and 'Abda and Fathi and all the other passengers?"

Talal responded, "Of course it could. The Good Lord could do it. You don't know Him!"

Next morning, my mother insisted on going with us to the Takhassusi Hospital to see Mounif.

"I want to see his face."

She kept repeating her demand and we didn't know if it would be a good or a bad thing. We went down to the basement where the hospital's refrigerators were located and our friend Dr. Barakat lifted the covering from his face. A strange feeling of tranquility and comfort came over me on seeing him return from exile and in the days that followed I discovered that everyone had been touched by the same tranquility and comfort, which is something I can't explain. It seems that news of the death in exile of someone living outside his homeland means basically that his family and those who love him will never see him again, as though he were just a news item, heard but not seen. As though, being no longer physically present anywhere, he was lost to them and they to him. As though he had been transformed from a body into an idea. When I saw his face, I felt I had discovered him over again and recovered him from the unknown. I went and touched him with my fingers, as my mother had done. This was his hair, this his brow, this his nose, and these his lips. This was Mounif with all his facial features, for real. We looked at him for the last time before pictures of him, hung on the walls, took his place in our house. My mother chose one picture and put it on the small table next to her bed and I'd often hear her talking to him in the early mornings—"Good morning, dear" in the mornings and "Happy feast day, dear" on the feasts—and she still talks to him from time to time; indeed, she consults him on decisions she intends to take, apparently genuinely waiting for answers. When I used to take her to her room at the end of the evening to sleep, I'd kiss her, cover her, put out the light, and say "Good night," leaving the door ajar as she didn't like it closed completely, and I'd hear her say, "Good night, dear." At such moments, I wouldn't know if she was talking to me or to the picture of Mounif.

At the hospital in Jericho, we say hello to the driver and get into the ambulance. Faisal and the doctor get in next to him and the nurse and I get in the back.

A sudden shudder runs through my body and I don't know where to look to avoid seeing what I just have.

My seat is on the oblong bench fixed to the right-hand wall of the vehicle, which is normally kept for nurses or those accompanying the patient, while the opposite wall is allocated to shelves for medicines and medical equipment. On the floor between the vehicle's closely spaced walls lies an old woman, her eyes opened to their widest, looking at me, and seemingly staring right into my eyes—mine and no one else's. Her skin is no more than a blackish coating, tightly stretched and clinging to the bones of the face. Her eyes maintain their stare; indeed, it seems to me that they follow me no matter where I move my head.

Minutes pass before I notice the medical tubes connected to this very thin, very long, body, which fills the entire length of the vehicle up to the back door.

The nurse sits down next to me, monitoring lines and numbers on the instruments fixed to the opposite wall. So she's alive. Why doesn't she lower her eyes? Why doesn't she make some movement to show that she's alive, and why won't she change the direction of that gaze of hers that keeps following me?

This time I am to enter Ramallah in the company of death.

As if death, like a creature of legend, were both outside and inside, behind the windows and in front of them. It seems impossible to get him out of one's mind. He's been in the city throughout the years of the Occupation and he's close at hand here in this ambulance. The nurse explains: "We have to run an MRI on her in Ramallah. She's being treated and there's a chance she'll get better, God willing. The poor woman contracted the disease while we were under siege. I just hope we find a place for her at Ramallah Hospital. Even the corridors are bursting at the seams with the martyrs and the wounded from this intifada."

Then he suddenly asks me a question that sends a chill through me: "Did you know Hussein al-Barghouti? He's from Kobar, but the Barghoutis are all one family so I expect you know him."

"Of course, God rest his soul."

It seems he hasn't heard my answer, because he proceeds to tell me about Hussein.

"God rest his soul—a poet, a university professor, a playwright, and a very nice-looking young man. I used to see him at Ramallah Hospital and took a liking to him. I was upset when he died."

The face of Hussein, who is gone and not gone, forces itself upon me.

The nurse realizes that I am no longer in the ambulance or following what he's saying.

Hussein al-Barghouti and I are sitting in the Ziryab Café, next to the elegant fireplace designed by our friend Taysir Barakat, the owner. There are a number of friends with us and Taysir has interrupted his fascinating discourse to welcome another guest or give instructions to his assistants. Others join us until our table looks like an open seminar next to the fireplace, where the wood crackles and the sparks dance as the Ramallah rains drench the city. Hussein smokes with relish as he discusses poetry, the novel, philosophy, and politics without a pause between sentences, as though afraid someone will interrupt him. He reminds me of the charming verse by Mayakovsky that goes,

The words exit my mouth
Like whores from a burning brothel.

That is how he usually was, but this time his manner seems strange—tense, and difficult to read. Taysir joins us and I tell him I like his new woodcarvings with which he's covered the walls of the café and ask him to give me a tour so that I can look at them more closely. Tasysir draws on wood using colors, carving, and burning; his talent is recognized by specialists and critics and has taken him to arts exhibitions in a number of countries around the world, always with success. He approaches life as though it will last a quarter of an hour, not more, loves to tell jokes, and has a fund of amusing adventures. He hiked from his birthplace of Gaza to Ramallah on a tour aimed at introducing him to the cities and villages of Palestine. As soon as he saw the mountains, he fell in love with them and their colors and contours and decided never to return to Gaza, which is as flat and tightly stretched as an ironed sheet. He picked up his paints and brushes and went around the villages, staying in any house that would take him in or renting a room wherever possible, painting, carving, sculpting, designing, and coloring. He put his artwork in the Ziryab Café in the heart of Ramallah, elevating the idea of café and restaurant to the level of gallery and cultural forum, which also gave him an opportunity to provide jobs for a number of young people. In the evenings, his wife and children join him for their almost daily family get-together. After we have moved away from the table and are on our own, I tell him I'm worried about Hussein, saying he doesn't seem normal that night and asking him if he knows anything I don't. As he is about to answer, a waiter comes to him for help with a problem, so I leave him to take care of his business. He turns back, though, and tells me in a low voice, "I'll explain later."

On my way back to Hussein's table, I notice Namiq al-Tijani sitting at a distance and feel an urge to vomit. I leave the place immediately and explain to Hussein from my cell phone that I saw the Namiq, felt disgusted, and left. He laughs and says to me, "That Namiq is going to haunt you. He'll never leave you alone if you don't take the decision to expel him from your head."

I do indeed run into Namiq al-Tijani everywhere and he does spoil everywhere for me. He seems to be more than just himself, more than just one person.

I become busy, don't return to the Ziryab Café for three or four days, and don't see Hussein. One day, I go out to look for a gift or a bunch of flowers to give to a lady who has invited me to eat fish for lunch having heard me singing the praises of fish on some occasion. At the crossroads in front of Rukab's shop I find myself face to face with Hussein, who is carrying his only child Athar in his arms and holding his wife Petra's hand. We greet one another and I ask him how he is. I don't tell him that I had been worried about him that evening at the Ziryab. I say only, "Put my mind at rest. Are you okay?"

"I wish I could say that."

I turn quickly to look at Petra's face in the hope of finding something in it that would show that perhaps he's joking but find her stony-faced and unaware that I'm looking at her.

"What do you mean?"

"You won't be reassured, my friend."

"You have bad news?"

"I have one of two possible things—AIDS or cancer."

. . .

"No, I swear it's the truth. Just as I told you."

"Come and let's sit down somewhere."

"No. The doctor told me that the symptoms that I was complaining of are . . . ."

Interrupting him, I say, "When did you go to the doctor?"

"A while ago. He said, 'We'll run some test for AIDS first and if they're negative, you have cancer.'"

. . .

. . .

"Are they running the tests?"

"Of course. What else could I do?"

"When are the results due?"

"In a week."

I look at Petra and Athar, and once more at Hussein. I say goodbye to them, do not continue on my way to lunch, and make my excuses to the lady.

The mountains of Kobar, its valleys and almond groves, as well as the streets of Ramallah and the corridors of universities, knew Hussein al-Barghouti by his long hair in falling curls around his exceptionally beautiful face, as also by his smile, his simple sandals, and his unkempt clothes, consisting usually of t-shirt and shorts. The cafes knew him from the gatherings at which he sat surrounded by students of his who loved literature and poetry and admired his writings and personality. No one knew him at Ramallah Hospital. He had to wait and receive the terrifying results from the hands of a female nurse with an expression bound to discourage optimism in anything that might originate from her.

Having found out that he'd been cleared of AIDS, he danced with joy . . . at having cancer.

Cancer was his own battle. It would never include his son Athar or his wife Petra.

When Athar was happy, he would 'tweedle'—"o-oh, o-oh, o-oh"—so Hussein took to jumping around the streets of Ramallah repeating "o-oh, o-oh, o-oh" and postponing that point in time—a point he had no desire to either name or fix—when he would take in properly the meaning of a confirmed diagnosis of cancer and at which he would begin his mythic preparation for death. We followed him as he "walked to his destiny alone," as he would write later in the book that reached me after his death and to which he gave the significant title *I Shall Be among the Almonds*:

I no longer have a place in this intifada beyond the boring routine of visits to the hospital, now my Kaaba or final Wailing Wall. The only space that can be made for me there is among the newborns on the top floor or in the refrigerator for the dead in the basement . . . . The wounded and the dead are everywhere, and I'm lost, asking for the hematologist. A harried nurse responds to my question with "Can't you see we're dealing with an emergency?" and I realize that I'm surplus to requirement, a parasitic patient walking to his destiny alone.

As I rewrote his death in my introduction to an Egyptian edition of his book, I did not mention the painful part of Hussein al-Barghouti's story, which is that some members of the family didn't recognize his value when alive. Some of them made fun of his 'womanish' hair, of his khaki Bermuda shorts, and of his habit of giving lectures in bare feet, and the poet was able to claim his place of honor among his family only through death. Even those writers who were consumed by jealousy at his skill competed over who loved him most in death.

The nurse is resting his head against the side of the ambulance, his eyes open, having graciously left me to my moment of withdrawal. The ambulance is taking the usual route from Jericho to Ramallah. There are no checkpoints on the road and everything appears to be going fine.

I can't take my eyes off the woman. I want her to come to, to utter a word, to complain how bad she feels, so that I can reassure her; to ask about her children, so I can tell her their news. Imagination takes me to one in the Gulf, another in prison, a third held up at the bridge. Impossible: it's clear she has no children and no husband. If my grandmother, Umm 'Ata, God rest her soul, had found herself in this situation while I was in Budapest, her daughter was in Amman, and her son was in Kuwait, would she be stretched out here like this woman? Is this woman, a stranger, lying here unconscious, aware that I now travel under her protection, that she is keeping me safe, colluding in my plans and collaborating with me, a child of her country whom she has never seen before and certainly will never see again from now till the end of time?

The ambulance stops suddenly and two Israeli soldiers approach.

To start with, one of them asks for the driver's papers. The two of them talk in Hebrew for a few minutes. Then the driver comes back and takes other papers from the ambulance and hands them over to the soldier, who examines them thoroughly. The soldier asks for the rear door of the vehicle to be opened. The two soldiers stand side by side but, before the driver can open the door all the way, they look, first into my face, and then into that of the sick woman. One of them, turning away, shouts, "Close door. Finish. Go from here."

The soldier hasn't been able to look at the face of the woman lying stretched out in the ambulance. We leave them and pass through. The nurse tells me, "You have the right glasses. They thought you were her doctor."

I think to myself, did this woman take part in the smuggling of two Palestinian writers without even knowing? When Faisal turns round to talk to me after we resume our journey, he sees her face and looks upset. I hear the doctor telling him what's wrong with her but can't make out his exact words. Faisal suffers from a slipped disc and I have chronic neck pain.

"To be honest, an ambulance is the right place for us. We're not infiltrators. You have an identity card and I have an identity card. We're citizens. But we're too old to put up with 'Qalandahar.'"

I laugh at the term, thinking it must be something Faisal has made up, but he explains that it's the people who have given the Qalandya checkpoint this name, derived from Qandahar in Afghanistan.

On our left, the settlement of Maale Adomim sprawls and spills over till it almost reaches the road. We're close to the Qalandya checkpoint now, though it hasn't appeared yet.

Suddenly I feel a dryness in my throat.

As though I'd swallowed dust.

No hand has throttled me but I feel as though a hand had throttled me.

It's the Wall.

The Wall, which separates Jerusalem from Ramallah and from all the lands of the Bank.

The Wall wasn't here last time. No news bulletin, statement of condemnation, official data as to its length, breadth, and height, or even photograph or television image, can convey its ugliness when seen by the eye. It's enough to see a person, any person, of flesh and blood walking next to the Wall to feel upset. That person doesn't have to be Palestinian, tired, wounded, an old man, a child, or in any way distressed to feel upset. Just seeing a person and this wall in the same frame is enough to send a shudder down one's spine. It's enough to see a cat prancing in its shadow or a nearby tree moved by the breeze or an empty can discarded at its foot to feel that nature—the air, winds, plants, weather—has been subjected to a cruel and disfiguring intervention. A thing of cement that winds its way among the houses, topped by army towers at irregular intervals. Reports, articles, speeches by politicians and campaigners for solidarity with the Palestinian people all speak of its disfigurement of the land. What I see, over and above that, is its disfigurement of the sky. Yes! This wall disfigures the sky itself. It disfigures the clouds that pass above it. It disfigures the rain that falls upon it. It disfigures the moonlight that touches it and the rays of the sun that fall next to it. The issue, however, certainly isn't only one of aesthetics. The Wall is surrounded by lies, some of which have been passed off on our worthless media, which repeats them idiotically. Lies such as that the Wall is a 'security' wall. The Wall has nothing to do with security. On the contrary, it is the wall of the great historic theft, the theft of more land and trees and water, the wall of the displacement of Palestinians following the exhaustion of their resources through their separation from their lands, crops, and water basins. It is built on land belonging to the Bank and if it were for security, as Israel claims, it would have been built along the 1967 borders. It is the wall for the emptying of the Bank of the greater part of its inhabitants through its inhibition of industry, agriculture, education, and geographical and social contact among people. It is the wall of the Silent Transfer. This wall puts houses in prison. Prisons the world over are designed for individual criminals who, justly or unjustly, have been found guilty. This wall has been designed to imprison an entire human community. To imprison a morning greeting between neighbors. To imprison a grandfather's dancing at his grandson's wedding. To imprison the handshakes exchanged at a ceremony of mourning for the death of a relative. To imprison the hand of a mother and prevent it from holding her daughter's when she gives birth. To separate the olive tree from the one who planted it, the student from his school, the patient from his doctor, the believer from his prayers at the mosque. It imprisons dates between teenagers. The Wall makes you long for colors. It makes you feel that you are living in a stage set, not in real life. It imprisons time inside place. The Wall is a word that has no definition except in the dictionary of death. It is the fear felt by our children and the fear felt by the others' state, for the Wall is the fear of both its sides. This is what makes it so satanic. International resolutions, court cases, the voices of Israeli peace advocates and of Israelis who believe in the right of the Palestinian people to freedom and self-determination will never bring this wall down, I tell myself. At the same time, I am confident that it will disappear one day by some other means. This wall will be demolished by our refusal to become used to it. It will be demolished by our astonishment at its existence. This wall will fall one day but now, in this moment of sorrow of mine, I see it as strong and immortal. The only things stronger than this wall are the birds, the flies, and the dust of the road. Then I tell myself, this is the Lesser Wall. The Greater Wall is the Occupation. Isn't the Occupation a wall too? I tell myself that I have lost all feeling. I tell myself, if nothing makes me cry any more, perhaps I would do better to laugh. And laughter would be easy: the victims of the ghettoes of the West reintroducing them in the East! In the third millennium, the Jews putting themselves in a ghetto again! And of their own free will, this time. Some of Israel's more intelligent politicians have said the same but no one has paid any attention. In the internal struggle over Israeli decision-making, the less intelligent side always wins—the side that sees the solution to all problems in 'absolute force.' And in the debate between the civilian and the military minds of the Jewish

State, the military always wins. This is the khaki state that throughout history has disliked colors. It is not enough that the Wall has no color; it also spoils all the colors around it. It spoils the embroidered dress of a peasant woman who waits four hours in front of one of its gates or beneath one of its towers. It spoils the school uniform of a small girl waiting impatiently for permission to get to her first class.

The Wall tempts its victims to jump it, if only in their dreams.

It tempts the strong and sturdy to wish that God had made them flying birds or climbing creepers.

It tempts one to infiltrate and penetrate it, as in a cartoon fantasy.

It tempts one to think of rock crushers, drills, and explosives.

It tempts one to make an unparalleled victory of the simple ability to move.

Israel has decided to put us in cans. Every crossroads is a cement can that we are stuffed into. Our movements, on the spot or in any direction, are hostage to a signal from their hand. Yes! A signal from their hand and no other. Otherwise, what would be the meaning of the Occupation? The Occupation is stagnation and the inhibition of movement to the point of paralysis. It is the inhibition of great ambitions and a decline into small dreams. It is the rejoicing of the oppressed over victories that dissipate as fast as hurrying clouds.

Yes! One of the things for which the Occupation will not be forgiven is its narrowing of its victims' ambitions. It hurls them, or most of them, into an abyss of small wishes and simple dreams. As a Palestinian whose will, like his land, is occupied—his history subjected to erasure and denial, the map of his country spread out on the table of the mighty masters, who have thrown on top of it a pair of super-charged metal scissors, ever ready to set to work—I fully realize that the repressed and oppressed of this world do not float high among the clouds of the sublime or of absolute beauty. They dig deep in the earth, looking for a living root, a viable shoot, a tree that may one day grow.

Yes! The existential crises so long that they turn to boredom, the daily aggressions that expand to fill decades, imprison their victims in simple dreams, such as the dream of crossing a street safely, of a child's reaching his primary school and returning from it on the school bus and not on the shoulders of his stunned schoolmates, of a safe stroll on the beach. The dream of there being anesthetic at the hospital, a glass of water when one is thirsty, a permit to visit the son in detention, idle chatter in the café, success in renewing one's passport, the ability to bury one's grandfather in his place of birth, to stay five minutes longer with the beloved, or to get the nod from a gum-chewing teenager in uniform to allow a lady to reach the maternity hospital before she's forced to deliver her baby at his feet. And just as a reminder, I say to those who are willing to listen, dreams become more dangerous when they are simple dreams.

The ambulance brings us to the place where the road divides.

The right arrow points to Ramallah.

The left arrow to Jerusalem.

This then is our promised 'Qalandahar.'

No one knows when the checkpoint will be working and when they will close it. Clearly, today it is working.

"We're lucky, Faisal. Inferno is open today. Prepare for the pleasure of entry, my friend."

"We have a long time ahead of us in Purgatory, Signor Alighieri."

"This Comedy is in no way divine. It's covered in mud, as you can see."

"Don't forget that this is the mud of the Holy Land. We can call it *The Muddy Divine Comedy*."

"And this is your crossing point to Paradise, Poet."

"Paradise Regained or Paradise Lost, Mr. Milton?"

"We're starting to talk nonsense."

131

"Yes, we're talking nonsense."

"Are we really?"

"No, the Holy Land is talking nonsense."

"The Holy Land or us?"

"We are the Holy Land."

"The Holy Land that's landed up in an ambulance."

"We're talking nonsense again."

"Yes, we're talking nonsense."

"But we aren't talking nonsense."

"If you want to be serious, we aren't talking nonsense."

"What are we doing now?"

"Talking nonsense."

"Do you think we'll go mad?"

"No. Don't worry. We're too cowardly for that."

"Long live courage."

"Long live cowardice."

"We're talking nonsense again."

"So what? What's wrong with that?"

"And what's right?"

"You're a man with a cause and a big-shot writer and you're talking nonsense?"

"What else do you expect from me when I'm creeping across the border in an ambulance like a mouse? Do you want me to roar? What do you want from me?"

"I want Godot."

"You're waiting for Godot and what you'll get is his brother, Shlomo."

Our travel companions thought that we really had gone mad, or become temporarily deranged. "Writers, dear God, and poets!" commented the doctor. "We deal with guts and scalpels but you're in a different universe. Watch out. We're close to the checkpoint. You never know, they may get it into their heads to check the mental capacities of people crossing at Qalandya as well."

The wait begins here. Hundreds of human beings standing outside their cars waiting their turn to be inspected. Car horns in short, sharp, pointless, stupid bursts. Some people smoke, some eat sandwiches wrapped in newspaper. Some curse and yell, and we still haven't reached the crossroads. Children and old people, the disabled and the sick, youths in jeans, girls wearing head coverings with jeans, fully veiled women, chic and would-be chic women with Gucci bags and high heels, peasants and old men and priests and business men and government employees and students. Psychologists say that crowding produces a 'hatred of the Other' and that that Other is the person standing in front of you in the line. You want him to get out of your way, to give you his place; in a word, you want him to disappear. This happens to humans and cars at rush hour and in front of cashiers' windows at the bank, the post office, and in airports. At Qalandya, the crowding makes you furious at yourself, at your countryman, and at the Occupation all at the same time. Boarding the buses at the bridge or getting off them, and in the bag inspection lines, your criticisms of your fellow citizens fly.

Why is she so fat? Why are they traveling with all that luggage?

Look, she's carrying a basket too! Why does that old woman have to bring blankets with her from Amman—aren't there any blankets in Palestine?

Why doesn't that idiotic child stop crying?

While all this is going through your head, you have no idea what the person standing behind you in the same line is saying about you. He too thinks you're dawdling deliberately and gets angry at you, not the one who's holding you up.

The long wait in the crush creates a need for many things, and needs create people to meet them. Purveyors of strange services multiply:

there's a wheel chair to transport the old, the sick, and the pregnant, or a porter with strong muscles who will do the job, and there's a lively donkey for hire too. These services are agreed to after tedious bargaining. A whole vegetable market has been spread out here, along with carts selling food, drinks, ice cream, tea, coffee, socks, cheap clothes, hats, falafel, kebab, children's toys, colored balloons, and more.

I realize we've arrived when I see the first tank, the barrel of its gun almost touching the mirror of our ambulance. Little by little, the entire martial scene reveals itself before us. More tanks are distributed on either side of the crossing point. Earthworks, rocks, and artificial mounds on either side of the road prevent anyone from leaving the asphalt. Everyone has to pass between the cement blocks, and over the heads of these hundreds flutters the flag of Israel with its six-pointed star. As though raising it in the air were not enough, they have also drawn it on the cement blocks.

The rows of cars have no end and there is nothing to gauge time by. Time here isn't measured by your wristwatch; it's measured by your ability to be patient. So long as you have the ability to be patient, time passes; when you lose it, it doesn't. The waiting leaves you rooted to the spot in front of its own dumb stupidity, like someone without eyes gazing at a non-existent picture of a billy goat hung on a non-existent wall.

Finally, we reach the heart of the checkpoint. We reach the 'heart of darkness.'

Fine rain has started to fall. One soldier stands close to us with his huge police dog while another asks for the driver's papers. He orders him quietly to open the door.

The scene is repeated. The soldier can't bring himself to look at the woman's face, with its open eyes and bared teeth. He allows us to go on our way.

We pass through the checkpoint.

We stop behind a car at the side of the road with its parking lights on. Abu Saji is waiting for us with his private car.

We get down from the ambulance with our bags. We say goodbye to the doctor, the driver, and the nurse. We thank them. They will continue their way to Ramallah Hospital to carry out tests on the woman. Faisal and I join Abu Saji in a hug.

"Welcome back. Hey! Big adventures at your age?"

"A lovely feeling of being wilier than the Occupation. We're just writers. We resist them with games like this and are happy when they don't catch us. What a journey!"

Abu Saji drives me to my hotel and takes Faisal with him. We've agreed to meet later at his house.

At the Royal Court Hotel, which looks out over Ramallah's park with its three cypresses in front, I take my sleeping clothes out of my bag, submerge myself in the warm water of the bathtub, lie stretched out luxuriating in the soap suds, close my eyes for a few instants, and see the woman laid out next to me on the stretcher staring at me with her wide-open eyes exactly as she was when we kept one another company in the ambulance. The nurse's voice rings in my ear: "There's a chance she'll be cured, God willing."

7

Saramago

On my way to the Khalil al-Sakakini Cultural Center, I catch a brief glimpse of him on the opposite pavement. It's Namiq al-Tijani. At first I feel depressed, then pessimistic, and finally alarmed at what may happen on a day that starts with a sighting of this hateful, slimy character.

He isn't one of the Authority's most corrupt figures. He's just a small one, a beginner, the likes of whom are to be found in their thousands everywhere. The sight of the big ones arouses only indifference now. Their corruption is firm, deeply rooted, and beyond redemption. There's no hope of their going straight: their corruption is classic, period. He, though, is a young graduate at the beginning of his career and it wasn't a given that he would become corrupt. The first group ended up corrupt and he began corrupt. His corruption is a blooming, fresh, rosy-cheeked corruption. A corruption strong of limb. A corruption that practices body-building. A corruption that massages itself if it can't find anyone else to do so. A corruption that works out in the morning and lunches well, not waiving its right to dessert (kanafeh from Nablus or tiramisu, baklava or cheesecake—anything sticky will fit the bill) to top off the already rich main course. It is a corruption with supple joints, strong bones, sharp vision, and a well-developed sense of smell that can catch the whiff of an opportunity from afar. A corruption that knows the directions and the roads and is quick on its feet. It is also an infectious corruption, quick to spread among those with the disposition and the propensity. The Namiq demeans himself in order to dominate. If you spit in his face, he will ponder the matter at his own speed, at his own sweet pace. Then, if the spittle has value, he'll collect it. He'll smile at you and if it was an act of gratuitous contempt, he'll count himself the winner and thank his good luck because you didn't kill him this time but contented yourself with spitting. When, however, in your absence, he's feeling secure, he'll allow himself all the time he needs to set a trap for you. This young man wants to get ahead, to make money, by any and all means. He no longer attracts attention because the line between ambition and greed has become thin and barely visible, but this young man's most vicious aspects are a tongue that extols and then betrays, a mouth that kisses and then bites, and a hand that embraces and then stabs. The likes of him are preparing themselves to be our future with the approval of the Authority. Against this, young people with clean hearts and heads are preparing themselves to be our future in spite of the Authority.

The Namiq crosses the street, approaching fast.

While a passing truck halts his forward rush, I enter the Center, climb the ancient stairs that lead to Mahmoud Darwish's room, and escape.

We had arranged this meeting in Amman, where I'd discussed with Darwish the program for a visit of the International Parliament of Writers and getting the building's conference hall ready for a planned press conference. The writers came, spoke, listened to the Palestinian writers, and expressed their solidarity with them and their desire to see the situation live, on the ground. We took them on a tour of the al-Am'ari refugee camp, which is in the center of Ramallah.

One of us had to explain to them who was taking refuge with whom, and how there came to be Palestinian refugee camps in Ramallah, which was Palestinian. Some of them weren't aware that these refugees were from the villages and cities of the Palestinian coast who had come here after their homes and possessions were destroyed following the Nakba of 1948. In other words, they had taken refuge in cities elsewhere in their homeland that were not occupied in the Nakba, and fled to the Bank and Gaza. They settled in nineteen camps in the Bank (a little later I shall explain the problem I have with the deliberately misleading term 'West Bank,' which poses a hidden danger): Balata, Tulkarm, Jenin, 'Askar, al-Diheishah, Shu'afat, al-Jalazon, Qalandya, al-'Arroub, Nur Shams, al-Fawwar, al-Far'a, Camp No. 1, 'Aqbat Jabar, 'Ayda, Deir 'Ammar, 'Ayn al-Sultan, Beit Jibrin, and the al-Am'ari Camp. This, of course, omits the Gaza camps, which will later take center stage in news bulletins because of the repeated Israeli attacks on their inhabitants; these are Jabalya, Rafah, Beach Camp, Nuseirat, Khan Yunis, al-Bureij, al-Maghazi, and Deir al-Balah. Others took refuge in Jordan, Syria, Lebanon, and elsewhere. Each bombardment or attack on these camps is, to their inhabitants, a second, third, or fourth Nakba. Israel's destruction machine drove them out of western Palestine, so they took refuge in its east.

What devilish thinking, then, led to eastern Palestine being called 'the West Bank'?

If you open the map of historic Palestine, you will find it located between the Mediterranean Sea on the west and the River Jordan on the east. The Zionist gangs occupied western Palestine, the country's Mediterranean coast, and most of its inhabitants took refuge in eastern Palestine, which extends to the River Jordan. Since the aim was to wipe the name 'Palestine' from the map, from history, and from memory, this area was attached to the River Jordan and called, in Arabic and every other language, 'the West Bank.' With this, the name 'Palestine' finally disappeared from the maps of the world.

If the west of the country is now called 'Israel' and the east is called 'the West Bank,' where is Palestine?

For Palestine to be lost as a land, it had to be lost as a word too.

Every time I hear the term 'West Bank,' I think of the enormous and deliberate pollution of language that has led to the assassination of the word 'Palestine.'

This is something the Chinese poet Bei Dao didn't know when he ran into a wall of denial in front of the Israeli Consulate in San Francisco. He told the young man standing there that he wanted to go to Palestine. The young man told him, "There is no such country on the map, sir!"

Later, PEN International Magazine will publish on its front cover—an undoubted honor—a complete poem of mine entitled "Interpretations":

A poet sits in a coffee shop, writing:
the old lady
thinks he is writing a letter to his mother,
the young woman
thinks he is writing a letter to his girlfriend,
the child
thinks he is drawing,
the businessman
thinks he is considering a deal,
the tourist
thinks he is writing a postcard,
the employee

thinks he is calculating his debts,
the secret policeman
walks slowly, toward him.

However, instead of writing in the list of contents 'Mourid Bargh-outi—Palestine," the magazine wrote "Mourid Barghouti—Palestinian Authority"!

When I asked them to explain, they said there was no country called Palestine, to which my response was, "Is the Palestinian Authority a country?"

Israel, then, is not the only party responsible for rubbing out the name of Palestine; it is the world. The Arab dictatorships have played, and go on playing, a larger role in this linguistic assassination than any other countries, including those of Europe and Israel's western allies. They are at least as much criminals in this as Israel.

I didn't explain all this to the writers' delegation as there wasn't enough time. I just wanted to point out that for sixty years the State of Israel has continued to pursue the refugees in their places of refuge. As a result, the massacres of the refugee camps bearing the names Jenin, Sabra and Shatila, Burj al-Barajneh, Tall al-Za'tar, and others have become a part of the background of the victim's double dispossession and murder. Yes! Double dispossession—otherwise, what is the meaning of the Occupation?

Here, in the al-Am'ari refugee camp, our guests and we saw the tactics the Israeli army had used to take it.

They would enter a house, arrest all its occupants, tie them up with rubber straps, and then use special explosives developed by Israel for such raids to make a huge hole in the wall shared with the next house and charge into that one. Palestinian families would be surprised by soldiers bursting through the wall, as in nightmares. Then they'd demolish another wall so as to break into the next house, killing those they wanted to kill and arresting those they wanted to arrest, and continue in this way from house to house and from hole to hole, the walls splitting open to reveal soldiers of the 'Defense Force' like in some Rambo film or Hollywood war. We and our guests passed through one of these holes like the soldiers and heard the local people's accounts of this repeatedly practiced form of attack. Some of them showed us the holes in the walls left by earlier attacks, which they had roughly repaired using basic materials.

When we toured the alleyways of the camp, one of the writers compared the Palestinian mothers standing in rows in front of their houses to the "chorus of women . . . of the Greek tragedies."

I thought to myself, this is the camp of the driver, Mahmoud. The moment we entered the place, his words "I'm from al-Am'ari camp" came to my ears. What had happened to him and his family? I thought I'd ask about him at his workplace the following morning, but in fact I didn't want to ask, so that I wouldn't hear an answer I didn't want to hear.

Army raids on houses in the cities are carried out by abducting someone and using him as a human shield. They force him to get into the tank—this once happened to my friend Husam—and then under the threat of their weapons make him press the bell of the house of a neighbor they want to arrest and call out his name. When the neighbors trustingly open the door, the soldiers burst in. All Husam could do was to go with his wife the next day to visit his neighbors and explain what had happened. He discovered that he didn't need to explain. The neighbors, like all the inhabitants of the city, had grown used to this method because it was used so often. On earlier occasions they had been used as he had.

We entered a school that functioned as al-Am'ari's computer training center and found the floor piled high with papers, plastic, wires, and cables. The computers were smashed and ripped open, the chairs smashed, and there were bullet holes in the walls. When we asked what had happened to the children, we were told that the army had taken them outside first and done them no harm. The objective had been to destroy the school and the computers, nothing else. Only someone who has experienced or heard of the experience of the Palestinians with education can understand what the destruction of a school in a camp means to the refugees. After the mass displacement in 1948 as a result of the Nakba, the refugees lived in tents set up for them in Jordan, Syria, and Lebanon by UNRWA, the refugee relief agency belonging to the United Nations, which provided them with just enough flour, cracked wheat, and sugar to keep them alive, plus some clothes. All of this was distributed in jute sacks, from which the refugees in turn made tatty robes and underwear. You would see the children in front of their tents with the flags of America, Britain, Canada, and other countries on their bottoms, over 'A Gift from Canada' or 'From the American People' or 'Point Four' (with its famous symbol of two hands clasping). Anyway, UNRWA refused to build schools for these children in spite of the insistence of their parents, who, though driven into poverty, had no desire to be driven into ignorance and illiteracy too. One of the first school teachers in the camps told me that he'd only managed to establish the first school there two full years after the Nakba, in 1950, when he put sixty pupils in a single tent. All UNRWA gave him for them were the chalk and the backboard. He brought a wooden notice board, wrote 'School' on it in Arabic and then again beneath it in English, and fixed the board to the top of a wooden pole, which he hammered into the ground outside. The children were fascinated by and fell in love with the school, which was paradise for them compared to the monotonous life of the camp.

The people of al-Am'ari camp were genuinely pained by the destruction of the computer center, though they quickly overcame that pain, as experience has taught them to do. In long conflicts, the weaker party experiences what might be called 'historical pain.' In such conflicts, the incident, the word, and the teardrop repeat themselves. Everything is repeated. Despair is repeated and hope is repeated. Heroism and treachery are repeated. Blood recurs and elegies recur. In long conflicts we don't have to wait for the massacre to experience the pain that will follow or for reality to come into being for art to be created. What we wrote in the past will always provide material that fits the future perfectly.

The cruelest degree of exile is invisibility, being forbidden to tell one's story for oneself. We, the Palestinian people, are narrated by our enemies, in keeping with their presence and our absence. They label us as it suits them. The weaker party in any conflict is allowed to scream, allowed to complain, allowed to weep, but never allowed to tell his own story. The conflict over the land becomes the conflict over the story and little by little the weak discovers that his enemy will not allow himself to be wronged. The enemy permits him only to be in the wrong, defective, and deserving of pain because he has brought that pain upon himself through his defects and his faults; it is not his enemy's doing. This is the cruelest form of injustice, and injustice is a form of exile, just as stereotyping is exile and misunderstanding is exile. In this sense, the entire Palestinian people is exiled through the absence of its story. On this visit a few of the writers of the world saw a few of the features of the Palestinian narrative and our exile became a little less acute.

I was walking with the writers and saw the mothers, the women's chorus of Greek tragedy, trying to protest to these foreigners, in a language they didn't know, against the cruelties of loss and the continuous repetition of killing.

In an interview with a radio station, Saramago said,

All the information I thought I had concerning the situation in Palestine has been destroyed. Information and pictures are one thing and reality is another. You have to put your feet on the ground to really understand what is happening there. All the world's bells have to be rung so that it can know that what is happening here is a crime that must stop. The Palestinian people are being subjected to unforgivable things.

But the world leapt to its feet— and still hasn't sat down again—in protest at Saramago's comparison in this interview of the crimes of the Israeli occupation with those of the Nazis, when he said that the Palestinians were living in a big concentration camp and compared Ramallah to Auschwitz.

Breyten Breytenbach was comfortable in comparing the situation to his experiences under the apartheid regime in his own country of South Africa, and the American novelist Russell Banks was angered by the fact that the soldiers of the Occupation looked like well-turned-out teenagers. "Look," he said, "that boy is doing his work more thoroughly than he needs to." (The well-turned-out soldier is examining the writer's IDs at the military checkpoint, his features empty of all expression.) What really got people worked up, though, was José Saramago and his comparison of Ramallah to Auschwitz.

Israeli politicians and literary figures, such as Amos Oz and A.B. Yehoshuah, along with most Israeli intellectuals (peace advocates until such time as their government makes war on us, when they become war advocates) went on the attack and accused him of anti-Semitism and 'moral blindness' while, far away, the Hungarian novelist Imre Kertesz popped his head up to add his voice, crowned with the laurels of the Nobel Prize, to that of those who had decided that Saramago was a "mediocre and failed" writer to begin with and anti-Semitic to the core. Some demanded the removal of his novels from the library shelves and a boycott of his publications, while the Israeli Foreign Ministry said that "Mr. Saramago has fallen victim to cheap Palestinian propaganda."

What was Saramago's response?

Saramago said,

"I'd rather fall victim to cheap Palestinian propaganda than to Israel's extremely expensive propaganda!"

Later, a few days after the writers' visit, when the Israeli army invades Jenin camp, and because of the presence of a limited number of Palestinian resistance fighters inside it, it will be bombed by Apaches and F-16s, which will succeed in wiping it off the face of the earth and the earth-movers and bulldozers will move in to demolish its houses over the heads of those inside.

The whole world will leap to its feet to protest the Jenin massacre but the moment America tells it to sit down, it sits.

The Security Council decides to send an international committee of investigation to uncover what happened in the camp.

The committee members reach Geneva on their way to Israel.

Israel announces it will refuse to receive them.

Things stop there. Just like that. It's over. And the delegation goes back home.

We go to Birzeit to visit the university. We cross the Surda checkpoint on foot, like the faculty and students of the university and the government employees, craftsmen, merchants, and sick of the neighboring villages. At the university we meet with the faculty members. After the meeting, the president asks us to write a few words and sign our names on a commemorative whiteboard. I'm standing next to Saramago, waiting for him to finish writing his contribution so that

I can write mine. I see him draw a rose and under it, in Portuguese, "The Palestinian State." Beneath that he writes, "A drop of water for this rose."

He signs it "José Saramago."

Dinner passes as big dinners do: side conversations that are never completed because they are interrupted by polite handshakes, words of introduction, and compliments, comments on the food, and a fair amount of gossip, including anecdotes concerning the behavior of this or that writer. The following day a meeting is organized at short notice with Yasser Arafat at his besieged headquarters in the Muqata'a building. Nothing new comes up, but the delegation notes the simplicity of his office and his frequent use of metaphors in his answers to their questions.

The office of the 'Palestinian President' is oblong and contains a number of seats, with an ordinary wooden desk to the right as one enters. This is piled with papers, files, medicines, and pens. Behind the desk is a plain wooden safe, on top of which numerous objects have been untidily thrown.

This is the third time I have entered a headquarters in which Yasser Arafat was living. The first was about a quarter of a century before, when I did so simply to perform a social duty: I was in Beirut and had to go with friends to offer condolences to Abu Lutf on the death of his brother. Arafat had opened his house for the occasion as a gesture of respect to his fellow PLO Executive Council member. The second time was when I came from Budapest to participate with the poets of the Arab countries in the Shaqif Poetry Festival in Beirut, held to salute the anniversary of the liberation from Israeli occupation of the fortress of al-Shaqif in southern Lebanon by the Lebanese-Palestinian Joint Forces—a truly heroic operation, in which the young men overran the towering citadel from their positions in the valleys and on the mountainsides. Among the writers invited were Sa'di Yusuf, Amal

Dongol, Mamdouh 'Udwan, Elias Khoury, Lami'a 'Abbas 'Amara, Yahya Yakhlif, and Radwa 'Ashour, who came from Cairo accompanied by Tamim, who was less than three. We were all invited to have lunch at Arafat's house. We took Tamim with us and Abu 'Ammar kept him on his lap the entire time; to this day, Tamim has the photo of him on his lap with poets Amal Dongol and Sa'di Yusuf and other Arab writers and Palestinian and Lebanese political leaders on either side. Today is my third visit.

This might seem normal were it not for the fact that Arafat kept open house for cadres of the PLO, Fatah, and other factions and parties. His house was also open for genuine fighters and people with serious political issues besides those who always sought financial help, a loan, an air ticket, money to cover the costs of a wedding, or an installment of a son's or daughter's university fees, all of whom wanted at the same time to gossip, slander, and tell tales. One of the main reasons for visiting him was to present financial requests and get them signed. Everyone knew his most famous expression, used when signing off on requests for assistance: "To be paid," above his signature.

Arafat liked to be asked for things and he liked those who asked. He suspected anyone who didn't want something material. I never attended an internal election that wasn't 'cooked,' openly, in front of my eyes and those of others, before it took place, always in order to arrive at a result that would please the president. When such electoral cookery was to take place, the president would know which cadres he could rely on; he gave to you and didn't forget, knowing that one day he would be able to count on you.

To this may be attributed the care he took to maintain his grip on the financial portfolio in any Fatah or PLO cabinet, in addition to being president of both organizations. I didn't approve of many of his policies, of his swapping kisses with the Arab rulers and his tendency to carry out their dictates, or of his reliance on bad elements to serve a cause that deserves the service of the best elements of our people. Despite all that, though, I, like the rest of the Palestinian people, viewed his mistakes not as those of a criminal but of a victim. He faced difficulties that would have crushed mountains.

In a kind of self-criticism, I say to myself: This was a leader of a liberation movement in exile, surrounded by twenty Arab regimes who viewed him as a threat, wanted him to fail, made alliances with his enemies, and tried to prevent him from speaking, acting, or moving. Who repeatedly waved their weapons in his face and chased his cadres and fighters from Jordan to Lebanon and from there to Yemen, Libya, Syria, and Sudan until the entire revolution was holed up in the Salwa Hotel in Tunis. He dodged and weaved and made all the right noises, offering a concession here to win a point there, and inevitably making mistakes—the mistakes, I repeat, of a victim and not of a criminal. Now here he was, living in the Muqata'a, under Israeli tank shelling and abandoned by every Arab ruler, some of whom refused even to take his calls, and I felt he belonged to me. I still ask myself the question asked by Naji al-'Ali's creation Hanthala—the question with which I concluded a poem of mine dedicated to the great artist twenty-five years before:

Father, O my father, how did you bring me to this place?
Father, O my father, how did you bring us to this place?

The Chinese poet Bei Dao asked him what had changed around him in the world, whose events he had lived through for decades. Arafat asked his assistant Abu Rudina to bring him a certain three-dimensional model. Abu Rudina couldn't find it, so he got up himself, begging pardon of his guests the writers, and fetched from the top of a wooden cupboard at the end of the room a model of a mosque, a church, and a synagogue. He told them, "I may be the only leader in the world who has a model like this in his office. The three religions are all here in my office."

The delegates appeared pleased.

"Another mistake," I thought to myself. "It's fine for him to take credit for religious tolerance as a general intellectual position, but who says our conflict with Israel is religious?"

The conflict didn't start in heaven and it won't be solved in heaven. It's a conflict over this land. It began because it was occupied and there will be no solution until that occupation ends.

Our problem with the Jew doesn't lie in his heaven, but in his helmet, which he claims is heaven, and in his rifle, which has been pointing at our heads for decades.

The Jew roofs his head with his helmet and the roof of a Palestinian house flies off. The Jewish settler's helmet is the Palestinian refugee's tent.

For thirty years, Arafat sank slowly into his mistakes, while his and our enemies urged him on in the hope that in the end he'd drown. His assistants and advisors, whom he had chosen, were unable to save him because all they'd learned from each new ordeal was how to save their own skins. His Palestinian opponents in other factions were too weak to resist his intrigues and tactics and so lost every round in their battle against the path he took.

Arafat was a master at demolishing his opponents but not at demolishing his enemies.

When we stood up to say goodbye at the end of the meeting, he asked us to wait a little.

He went to his desk at the other end of the room, squatted down to search though the drawers for something, and then returned, his hands full of small, square boxes that he hugged to his chest to prevent from falling. He started opening the boxes one by one and taking out small, ordinary-looking pins, one of which he stuck onto the chest of each of his guests, as though it were the highest of decorations.

When it was my turn I examined the one he gave me closely.

It was a round plastic badge, about as small as a piastre coin, on which was written "Bethlehem 2000." Bethlehem 2000 was a tourism project to prepare that city for the third millennium celebrations, and had been over and done with for two years. The pins that he distributed to his guests were obviously the remaining few of thousands that the city's residents and visitors had stuck on their chests for that occasion. He had wanted to give a presidential souvenir to his guests but, imprisoned as he was by this siege that had turned a loaf of bread or a cup of water into a rarity, could find nothing other than this humble plastic pin. Despite this, Arafat presented the pins with the flourish of the host who has little to offer but "makes a feast of whatever's to hand" and the grace of one who is never at a loss, no matter how difficult the circumstances.

Later, when the news of his death reaches us while I'm on a literary tour in "the most beautiful spot in the English countryside," near Hadrian's Wall, I will inform the tour's organizer that I want to return to London the next morning and I do so.

I cut short my tour and returned on my own to London, not to do anything particular but because, quite simply, I couldn't remain in "the most beautiful spot in the English countryside" on a day like that.

The long reel turned in my mind. This Arab leader, whose food was worse than my food, whose drink was worse than my drink, whose clothes were less elegant than my clothes, whose picture was hung on a shattered wall framed by the roar of the missiles, bombs, and bullets aimed at him, was abandoned in the night of his headquarters—lit by one, or two, candles discovered somewhere by accident—by every other Arab leader. They didn't send him a loaf of bread or a glass of water. They didn't ask Sharon to lift the siege. In fact, because of their policy of collaboration with Israeli and American policy, they continued to pressure him, pushing him into making concession after concession. His error in signing the Oslo Agreement was only one of the results of their pressure on him and of his despair that any good could come from these quaking regimes, afflicted with the sickness I call "the fear of victory."

These were the leaders who had competed so hard to have their picture taken standing next to him so as to gain the affection of their people by playing the Palestinian card. The issue was no longer 'political' for me; it had become at times an existential scene and at others a demonstration of men's destinies and the turning of Fortuna's wheel, casting those destinies down from zenith to nadir. It was the same scene that has filled the shelves of libraries with Greek tragedies, whose sad hymns, sung by choruses of ill-tidings and bad omens, make nature tremble, and which have taught men's hands the meaning of the lowering of the curtain in the fifth act.

The helicopter carried him from the courtyard of the Muqata'a to his hospital in Paris. Like a child he distributed kisses into the air to its right and left, with a strange repetitiveness. They were the same kisses that had saved him so many times in his life before when he had planted them on the cheeks of the very leaders who had been afraid to get close to him out of fear of the Master in his White House, leaders who believed the eternal charge of terrorism that had been attached to him and his whole people so that justice could maintain its contrived absence. Justice does not disappear by coincidence. It disappears only beneath a military boot or a silent tongue. These kisses of his were now kisses for his people, who came out to bid him farewell on his journey to the cure that in the end failed to cure him.

I, the simple citizen who didn't support his policies, was comfortably ensconced in "the most beautiful spot in the English countryside," while he was in the hands of his doctors and needed a gulp of air, while he was in his shroud and needed two meters of land in his city of Jerusalem so that its earth might gather his short body and long story into its memory. But he was also the only Arab 'president' to say no to the most powerful nation in the world, a president who refused to abdicate and who died a suspicious death whose secret will come out only with a major advance in the science of poisons.

Some saw him as a father. I didn't see him as a father in any way. I reject in principle the idea of the leader as a father. I reject the idea of citizens as 'children' and I reject the idea of the nation being 'a family.'

All the same, his simple death was too complex for me to accept as one does life's recurrent rites. I feel a degree of guilt and regret for my earlier stands and of perplexity over how to define his historical legacy and put a precise name to what history will retain of him.

Wait, though. He played his role as a politician who sometimes got things right and sometimes got them wrong, and I played what I believe is the role of the citizen, which is not restricted to applause.

The humanity of a leader doesn't show in how he carries on the game of politics; it shows in those moments when politics are absent. He would visit us at Broadcasting House in Cairo and everyone would have falafel for lunch, the patties spread out on newspaper or the drafts of the political commentaries we'd prepared for the microphone in the hope that they'd set fire to the ground beneath the Occupation's feet and ignite the Revolution in the breasts of the Palestinians. If we decided to celebrate, lunch would be fried fish from a restaurant that delivered, with plastic knives and forks that broke at the first bite, so that we'd end up using our hands instead. We'd drink water from paper or plastic cups, standing in line in front of a miserable tap in the broadcasting service's poverty-stricken building, before continuing our conversation and he'd say things, some of which we liked and some of which we didn't. I used to say to my colleagues at the Voice of Palestine, "If this man succeeds in bringing an end to the Occupation and becomes president of our 'independent Palestinian republic,' he'll be the only one in the Arab world to have gained his position by right of struggle, sweat, and long nights, and not by a coup, a rigged election, a referendum whose results are known beforehand, or the support of the CIA and the Pentagon." So what happened?

The Oslo Agreement bestowed on him a photocopy of the position of president. And now he's escaped the siege for an eternal absence, and Palestine is still waiting. And it will be a painful wait, more painful perhaps than the man imagined.

The real catastrophe for the Palestinians these days is that they find themselves under the leadership of the pupils in the absence of the master.

At the hands of these pupils and thanks to their erratic stumbling around between the national project and their inability to defend it, the Palestinian Authority has turned into a huge NGO living off the financial assistance of the European countries, while Europe fails to realize that through its expenditures on the Palestinian Authority it simply finances and prolongs the Israeli military occupation. Israel occupies the country, Europe pays the costs of that occupation, and the Authority implements Israel's conditions. Yes! From a liberation movement of stubborn persistence it has tuned into a fat, flabby NGO at which they brandish the stick and the carrot and which out of fear of the first pants naively after the second, unaware that throughout history it is precisely the carrot that has embodied the underhandedness of imperialism. No one swallows the stick, because they're afraid of choking on it. Indeed, the stick may incite resistance, endurance, and defiance, and make one search for the sources of one's strength in order, at least, to defend oneself. It is the carrot that is the real threat. The carrot is smooth, soft, and tasty at one end; little by little, however, as one moves toward the other, it gets thicker, coarser, and woodier. The imperialist carrot is in fact the real stick.

This is what the Authority hasn't learned.

This Authority walks, and sometimes runs energetically, sincerely, and self-sacrificingly, after a poisoned chalice but trips over the hem of its drawers and falls down at every step. When it gets back up and tries to resume its progress, it finds it has distanced itself from the people, ignored their small, pressing needs, is now worlds apart from them, and has lost control of even its own helpers and supporters. Distance from and contempt for the people as individuals is a recipe for disaster in any political action. There is near consensus among Palestinians that the armed and bloody infighting between Fatah and Hamas would not have occurred if Arafat had been alive. This is not because he was a saint, for even a saint can't still be a saint after forty continuous years in power and is bound to commit a series of mistakes and sins—and Arafat may have committed many or few—but because Arafat knew how to keep control of his aides no matter how far they might go, and how to take the wind out of the sails of his opponents in the other factions. Bloody civil war wasn't part of Arafat's political vocabulary, even if events may sometimes have taken him to its brink.

The next day was my meeting with Marwan al-Barghouti. I discovered that the absence of Marwan—an excellent reader and follower of political and literary writings in the Arab world—from our international writers program had been due to security concerns, but that he had followed the stands and statements of Christian Salmon, Wole Soyinka, Breyten Breytenbach, Saramago, and Consolo from his place of hiding. He spoke at length of the need for Palestine to become once more the point of convergence for people of conscience the world over.

Neither he nor I then knew that a few days later he'd be arrested, to disappear under a long sentence into the prisons of the Occupation, and that Palestine would lose the efforts of one of its honest men.

The most beautiful event of the writers' visit took place at the Qasaba Theater in Ramallah with the evening of joint readings by Palestinians poets and the guest writers. The star of the evening was the audience, which exceeded a thousand women and men who had come to the theater from every part of the Bank, despite the siege. Despite the dangers and annoyances of the checkpoints, they stayed on till midnight, for the poetry and the literature and to welcome the writers as their guests. The audience listened to readings in languages they did not know with such respect and enjoyment that one could have heard a pin drop, and by the end of the evening they were so taken by its magic that they stood and applauded for many minutes. The Qasaba Theater and Cinema Club was formerly a beautiful old cinema close to our house in the Liftawi Building; the director and actor George Ibrahim has converted it into its present elegant form. The people of Ramallah have taken the place to their hearts and professional and amateur theater troupes have been active in presenting their varied works on its stage.

Later, almost immediately after this rare writers' evening and just three days after the writers had left, Israeli tanks will force their way into the city of Ramallah and vandalize the Qasaba. The soldiers will enter and destroy the sets, backdrops, curtains, and seats while the echoes of our readings and those of our guests are still reverberating in its air. One journalist wrote of this incident that "it was as though they were trying to destroy any possibility of the resumption of speech."

They also broke into the building of the Ministry of Culture, a tall block overlooking Arafat's headquarters, and destroyed it, leaving it full of filth. They would repeat the same acts in all the cities of the 'West' Bank, leaving our dead on the doorsteps of their homes.

What scares me most is that we might get used to the idea of death, as though it were our unique lot or the only result that we have to expect from any confrontation. I want us to think, with each of

death's victories, of the magnificence of life. In a poem I will write
later, I ask myself,

Why, when I see a dead man stretched out on the ground,
Do I believe it's someone thinking?

At the end of the visit, at a meeting between the guest writers and
Israeli writers of all persuasions, the words of the well-known Israeli
writer and activist Yehudit Harel—as communicated by the news
agencies to those of us who weren't there—seemed the most daring
and clear. In defending Saramago and attacking his critics among
the Israeli intelligentsia, she said, "Perhaps there never really was
an 'Israeli peace camp.' Even if we suppose the opposite, we now
know for sure that it vanished two years ago, probably because of the
misuse of words and because of the idea that dominates our thinking
specifically that makes us speak of ourselves and of the Palestinians as
though we are moving in a vicious circle of mutual violence, for which
the responsibility falls on both parties equally."

Yehudit Harel went on to say, "I wish to protest against this false
balance and this abuse of language. The circle of violence is not formed
of two equal sides. One side is the Occupier and the other is the victim
of our occupation. Nevertheless, we still apply the word 'violence'
to every outburst of Palestinian resistance, to every battle for liberation to which they have recourse, and to every act of resistance to our
occupation. This is not violence. It is legitimate rebellion."

Later, the visit will be documented in a film called *Writers on the
Borders*, which ends with Yehudit Harel's plea to this delegation of
people of letters from every corner of the world: "I trust in you, when
you return to your countries, to help us rid ourselves of these dishonest
mythologies, of which we have become ourselves the victims."

8

The Alhambra

The moment he opened the door of the apartment to me to show me around, I was assaulted by the color red—the wall-to-wall carpeting was red and on it squatted a large couch with, arranged around it, four chairs of the sort that are almost too heavy to move. These were red too. The curtains were (by way of a change) pink. The bedroom was brown and had a balcony that looked out over a kitchen garden in which were a mulberry tree, a loquat tree, a lemon tree, and a spacious old single-story house. The kitchen was a reasonable size and from it a wide passageway led to a surprisingly elegant bathroom. From the neighbors' kitchen garden rose the voice of Fayrouz:

> *Give him my greetings*
> *And tell him that I greet him,*
> *You who understand his ways.*
> *Greet him from me,*
> *Greet him.*

Then I heard the sound of a piano trying to pick out the song; the player was clearly just a beginner. I decided to take the apartment. Next day I fetched my suitcase from the Yasmin Building and took up residence in what I would call 'the Alhambra.' I went to a shop to buy houseplants and picked out a tall bush with dense elongated leaves like those of a mango. I asked where it was from and the salesman told me Thailand and gave me its difficult name, which I forgot despite my best attempts. I put it in the corner of the living room closest to the window, where it was the only thing in the furnished apartment that I owned and had chosen for myself, and it immediately claimed me as its owner. It grew fast, as did our friendly, familiar, and sociable relationship.

I took up my duties at the foundation.

I observed the Namiq and his doings firsthand. I don't need to go into detail as the Namiq is himself the detail. The Namiq is an indestructible survivor, because he has fashioned himself to fit the preferences of the Authority and the Authority has fashioned the Namiq to fit its preferences. The Namiqs returning from Tunis sought out the resident Namiqs and extended their hands to them, along with opportunities and profits. Thus was formed the alliance that is the last and worst thing that a liberation movement needs. I had agreed to be director of the foundation for a year and from the first weeks it became obvious that it was consumed from the inside by financial corruption—falsified invoices, salaries for non-existent employees, allowances, per diems for journeys never made, and seventy employees to do work that needed twenty at most. As usual, corruption won, albeit only partially this time. I tried and neither succeeded totally nor failed totally. In the current delicate Palestinian situation, this must be considered total failure.

Life teaches us a lesson that cannot be ignored: it isn't enough for some of the players in the orchestra to do their work well; it's either collective excellence or cacophony. If that's true of music, how much more so must it be when an entire people wishes to bring life itself back from its hiding place, so they can know it and live it?

I placed a pile of forged and suspect invoices on the table of the project's financial director and asked him to take the necessary steps vis-à-vis the payees. He advised me to sign them for payment.

I presented my resignation, which was refused, so I called a meeting where I said, "I am the weakest person at this meeting. I have no party, no faction, no one in what you call 'the government' to protect me, and no clique anywhere to support me. But I do have this" and I raised my pen in my right hand for all of them to see.

The next day, I went into my office and could hardly recognize it.

A set of black leather chairs.

New curtains,

A new computer,

A laser printer,

A new carpet.

They were running a test. Would a new office be enough to make him shut up?

I presented my resignation and left for Amman the same day without waiting for a reply.

After numerous intercessions from persons I respect who promised to bring pressure to bear to improve things, I reluctantly returned after thirty-five days of absence.

Things changed for the better for two or three months and then the collusion with theft started again. The end of the project brought true relief. By the time I returned to Cairo, any hope I might have had that things would straighten themselves out under this Authority had vanished.

My residence in Ramallah for a number of successive months (the period of my protest resignation excluded) had allowed me to observe the political and economic kitchen from the inside, and what I'd seen wasn't pretty. I told myself that my chronic opposition had been totally justified and I'd been unjust to none. I had upbraided myself for my isolation and my dedication to reading and writing but now, after having been granted this further opportunity to experience government practice from the inside, I decided to respect my voluntary isolation and maintain it forevermore.

This time I returned to my isolation with an easy conscience.

The Namiqs will continue to be masters of the hidden and the public world and this will last forever.

My near daily battles to stop the squandering of money made me enemies, who would fight me with a look, or words, or by trying to do me harm. Those who should have cared and whom I asked for support demonstrated their expertise at evasion and flight. I stopped asking them for anything.

Once more I depart.

Once more I withdraw.

Once more I flee.

Once more I'm too much of a coward to butt heads with the bastards.

I say a thing and its opposite at one and the same time. I tell myself I'm a coward and not strong enough to butt heads with them. Then I say that I'm not a bull that I should charge other bulls and that I refuse to be made into a bull. I want to accept the situation like a proper man or oppose it like a proper man.

The Namiqs won't allow your humanity to function. They want you to be either a hopeless floor rag or a hopeless monster and I'm neither the one nor the other. My withdrawal may place me outside events, but I'm certain that the homeland won't be liberated by either a floor rag or a monster.

This time I withdraw without regret. It amazes me that Israel doesn't abandon its attacks and random killings. It's as though it doesn't want to facilitate the success of the Namiq party in the Authority's activities. It strikes the 'moderates' with the same viciousness as the 'hardliners' and doesn't let either camp achieve anything that it could offer the people as a justification for continuing to rule in their name.

During this period, I made the decision to organize my work so that it didn't take the pleasure out of my whole day. I took the evenings for myself, and weekend mornings the same. On those mornings I would go out to the Upside Down café in front of Ramallah Park and have my coffee and breakfast before setting the program for my day.

It was a cloudy morning in February. The sky, which was the color of white grapes, was low, and the fine rain had the demeanor of a placid guest. My gaze shifted from the piece of paper in front of me on the table to the three towering cypresses at the entrance to Ramallah Park and back. Every time I set myself to work on something, it would escape me and gradually fade away and I'd be once more like someone kidnapped by fairies, gazing at the cypresses as though something was puzzling me.

That's how it usually is: when your eyes delete all the objects in your field of vision and leave only one, that object arrests their entire attention, and that object, which is now the only thing you can see, is your next passion or your next poem.

Suddenly,

That music that never emanates from any visible source engulfed me.

So it's a poem.

It's poetry.

I ask the waiter for blank paper and a cup of coffee and to lower the volume of Umm Kulthoum's voice a little, which he does.

I take out my pen and start writing:

> *Transparent and frail,*
> *like the slumber of woodcutters,*
> *serene, portending things to come,*
> *the morning drizzle does not conceal*
> *these three cypresses on the slope.*
> *Their details belie their sameness,*
> *their radiance confirms it.*
> *I said:*
> *I wouldn't dare to keep looking at them,*
> *there is a beauty that takes away our daring,*
> *there are times when courage fades away.*
> *The clouds rolling high above*
> *change the form of the cypresses.*
> *The birds flying toward alternative skies*
> *change the resonance of the cypresses.*
> *The tiled line behind them*
> *fixes the greenness of the cypresses*
> *and there are trees whose only fruit is greenness.*
> *Yesterday, in my sudden cheerfulness,*
> *I saw their immortality.*
> *Today, in my sudden sorrow,*
> *I saw the axe.*

I went to Amman once every one or two months.

I'd spend Thursday evening and Friday with my mother. She'd see me and I'd see her and we'd be reassured. I'd return to Ramallah before noon on Saturday and be in my office on Sunday morning.

Those months spent between Ramallah and Amman were months of poems, or beginnings of poems. I lived in a state of love with the autumnal and wintry weather in the hills and valleys of Ramallah and with the two gardens of the house in Amman. I adore the winter and the rain and the trees and I adore the light of the world at eleven o'clock in the morning under the fine rain, with the song "Give Him My Greetings" and Luciano Pavarotti, and I adore having the draft of a new poem on my desk in front of me and adding or erasing lines.

I am one who loves the sound of rain on something hard. When thunder and lightening come with the rain, I feel a need to do something. I go out onto the street without an umbrella, I jump and cry out and yell like a fool, and I return to the warmth of my room, bringing with me an intoxication that my body can't contain and I don't know what to do with.

One winter the snow fell thickly, so Muhammad, my brother 'Alaa's son, and I went out to play in it. I was surprised to find him yelling, running, and turning circles with evident joy. He hadn't seen snow since he was a child because he'd been living in the Gulf with his parents and had only recently come to join the University of Jordan in Amman. I was surprised to hear him ask me as he leapt and laughed—or perhaps he was really asking himself—"Uncle Mourid, what are you supposed to do when you're happy?"

I looked at him in astonishment. He added, "Seriously. I'm happy and don't know what to do about it."

The path to my white office in my mother's house in Amman is lined with lavender, ivy, rosemary, bird-of-paradise flowers, geraniums, jasmine, and one short palm tree—a raised garden on whose left a flight of steps leads to my garden at a lower level. The sound of shoes coming down the steps alerts me to visitors, the thought of some making me overjoyed, of others miserable. The burden of keeping away visitors I don't wish to see has fallen on my mother.

"He's writing."

I put the mighty-bodied Pavarotti into the tape recorder and let the ecstasy he brings play tug of war with me, my world, and the rest of the world, toppling us head over heels into pleasure, the three of us rolling around on the ground of secrets and in the seductiveness of poetry. Not my family, nor my readers, nor the street, nor the windows surrounding the house, nor anyone in the whole city knows what Pavarotti does to this white room. His firm voice is a bronze hand that pushes me to write and legs on which I run in a daze from which I wake when I crash into a tree that is naked of all but birds, a tree with a voice and huge wings on either side. The voice of the tree seduces me into listening to my voice, which is hidden at a depth of which I am aware only when I make it a written voice, a voice that throws me into its forest and leaves me to find my way among the shadows and lights and unexpected beasts that lurk among them. I see a naked gazelle I see a lofty tree I see broken spears I see panthers yowling at their mates I see a single jasmine flower on black satin. I see a red that is hot to the touch I see holes in the earth waiting for their tenants to be borne to them with terrifying solemnity.

Here I feel joy, sadness, and fear. I hate my loneliness and I love it and long to leave and long to stay, so I do not truly leave and do not truly stay and am become more than my body.

I begin my day at five in the morning with a tour of the trees and rose bushes in the garden, shears in hand—not to harm them but to grant them the life they need to bloom. If we don't cut the roses from the branches, the bush will stop doing the only job it does well—the rose.

I return to the bath tub and its soapy hills, after adding lavender or bay or rosemary leaves and sometimes sprigs of the pepper plant, mint, pelargonium, or sage, and sometimes all of them together. I follow this with a very hot shower followed by a very cold one, as I have done for years beyond numbering, even if snow blankets the world outdoors.

After this, I go upstairs to join my mother for our morning coffee and listen to the plan for her day. Usually she starts with her standard question, "What shall I cook for you today?" I answer straight away with the name of some dish and she feels a sense of great repose. The thing a mother least wants to hear in answer to that question is "Whatever you like" or "It doesn't matter" or "Anything" and I've learned to name the day's dish for her quickly and without hesitation. After the morning chat, I take my leave of her, return to my office downstairs, and sit down to reconnoitre the possibility of writing.

I may write two lines or two pages or the sheets of paper may stay white and unblemished. Poetry is like love, like the world, like the unknown destiny of man—rough or smooth, and sometimes rough and smooth together, and the rough talks to the smooth in the poem the way the drums talk to the flutes in the orchestra. In this way the poem conceals what it wants in order to reveal it more clearly.

In spite of the difficulty of what I try to do, I love to write poems using the softest possible voice, even while they preserve the roughness of the history that fills poets' bodies, their rooms, and their memories, which are sharp as Swiss knives. The heroic tone in the tyrant's voice has helped me rid myself of poetic heroics. The fierce Italian has saved my poetry from fierceness.

In the red Alhambra, I finish the poems that are born here in my white office, and what is born in the Alhambra or at the Upside Down café in front of the park I finish in Amman and Cairo.

I cannot calculate how much I've written with my eraser, for I have torn up much and regretted much. How happy I've been at my eraser's cruelty! Doesn't deleting give as much pleasure as writing?

What does writing get its value from if not from what we have deliberately erased . . . so that it stands out more clearly?

The tree that bears a thousand buds resolutely and without hesitation abandons many of its fruits and allows them to fall dead next to its trunk so that it may take better care of the rest.

Trees fascinate me not just for their beauty but because I see in them also a symbol of resistance without bluster or bragging. It fascinates me too that the unarmed tree knows that everything that is permanent is temporary.

Come and see:
Their nakedness shudders silently beneath the whip of the
wind.
Birds dare not visit them on their silent war front,
nor bees.

One clever branch tells another:
"Slow down!
This is no time for greening, hot head."
The branch nods to its friend, with an obedience
As complete as the surrounding emptiness.

The trees look like bombed out villages abandoned by their
inhabitants
Who have taken with them their colors, their breezes, and
their shadows
And left them surrounded by roaring hardships.

No one is left to share their moans beneath the blows of the
thunder
And the electric torture sessions of the lightning.

Come and see:
 And because many do not look at a field that is clothed in
nothing,
 Because the great do not disclose their mysteries,
 Because the trees, like us, are fighting an alliance of the
snows of the north,
 The fog of the gods,
 And the lack of a helping hand,
 And because all probabilities are open,
 Come now. Come and see:
 Teach your heart to trust their silence,
 Which resembles ours.

Come and see:
 The trees, which, like us, looked dead or almost so,
 Were fighting all the time!

 And on a known day,
 At the one and only appointed time
 And because nothing is ashamed when its time is come,
 The clever branch says:
 Now! Now, companions,
 Now, enduring, patient branches,
 Now
 Let us proclaim our spring.

 The kingdom of leaves
 Opens its doors to the birds, to the bees,
 And we humans prepare the baskets.

 And on a known day,

The stage hand raises the curtain:

The basket of fruits at the center of the homely scene
Blazes
Like victory.

The Alhambra was the second place in which I'd lived on my own after my time alone in Budapest. I had a year ahead of me to perfect my solitude once more. It wouldn't take much training. I have enough experience of solitude to open an institute.

The list of friends grew longer by the day, as did the list of relatives with whom I renewed acquaintance after my long absence in distant countries. But definitely I was in love with the new-old place. Long walks among the trees and on the hills, and getting to know the gardens of the houses with their lemon, orange, mandarin, and loquat trees, was a pleasure surpassed only by that of stealing one or two figs cut from the branches close to the street, and the sensation of the smell of jasmine that rose from the walls and spread to the four corners of the earth, filling my whole body and my chest.

It made me happy.

And, excited by that vital mixture, the writing squirmed inside me as though kicking me with its feet. Even though I didn't know its name and sex, it was a life coming from the future and wanting to emerge into the present.

I had constructed my own Upside Down café for my writing here just as I had constructed my own Zsolnay Café in Budapest. Here, in the Alhambra, I used Fayrouz and Pavarotti; at the Upside Down, there was Umm Kulthoum. At the Zsolnay, there was Mme. Gabriella, the seventy-year old pianist, who would greet me with Beethoven's *Für Elise* as soon as I entered. I'd send her, via the waiter, a glass of Rémy Martin in acknowledgement and she'd put it on the edge of the piano, where the cognac would remain unshaken no matter how loud the music at the crests of the crescendo. She would thank me with a nod and a calm smile and move on to Rachmaninov, Chopin, and the rest of her daily program. I'd sit down and the waiter would set before me a pen, blank sheets of paper, and a cup of coffee with a piece of the café's special chocolate on the saucer, leaving it up to me to order anything else I might want after that. I would write, erase, rip, and keep only a little, but I'd return carrying a draft that I could work on through the night.

Summer arrived. Tamim came to Ramallah to spend a few days with me before joining Radwa in Amman, where she would arrive with the start of the university vacation. This time he came on his own. And this time too he got in easily.

I went with him to all the places I had formerly known in Ramallah and al-Bireh, and to new ones too.

Some of his poems had been published in the newspaper *al-Ayyam* and when he visited the House of Poetry, they offered to publish his first collection of verse in Palestinian dialect. He handed over to them his collection *Mijana*, and was both scared and happy.

Unexpectedly, I received some good news.

9

Things One Would Never Think Of

nis came to me and said he'd been given the task of organizing a conference of Palestinian expatriates in Ramallah and that my brother Majid was among those invited. Incredulously, I said to Anis, "But he doesn't have a Palestinian identity card, so how will the Israelis allow him in?"

"We're going to get week-long visitors' permits for all the invitees."

"They've agreed to that?"

"They've agreed."

"When's the conference?"

"Next week."

Majid came from Doha to Amman. There our mother decided to come with him, to see me, Ramallah, and Deir Ghassanah.

On the promised day, I asked Tamim to go to Amman to accompany his grandmother and uncle on the journey. I took him as far as Jericho and he went on to Amman. Then the three of them returned together and the Alhambra was brought to life.

Majid, who hadn't seen Ramallah since he'd gone there clandestinely on foot after the occupation in 1967, was in seventh heaven.

I had to make a great effort to prevent my mother from getting engrossed in straightening up the apartment and making improvements.

Nothing about my rented apartment pleased her. The kitchen was "the size of a needle's eye," of course. The living room set was "commercial furniture" and the arrangement of the chairs was "wrong—this way's better." She asked me to buy new kitchen equipment and whatnot. When she learned that I ate in restaurants, she said pityingly, "Restaurant food will make you sick, you poor thing. What could be better than home cooking?"

"You're my guest. I'm the one who's going to cook and do the washing up and clean the house. Okay?"

"It won't do, my son."

"It will and that's it."

She smiled like one who doesn't want to hear.

Majid was only nine months old when the Nakba occurred in 1948 (even my youngest brother is nine months older than the State of Israel). We were living in the city of Lydda, where my father worked, and there Majid was born in 1947, his birth bringing the number of brothers to three—Mounif, the eldest, who was born in Jericho, then me, who was born in Deir Ghassanah, then Majid. The attacks on Lydda by armed Zionists struck terror into the hearts of its inhabitants, not to mention the news that reached them of the killings and forced migration to which the other Palestinian cities, towns, and villages up and down the coast had been subjected. Reports of the hundreds of thousands who had fled by boat to Gaza or on foot to Lebanon, Syria, and Jordan came in quick succession. My father decided to take us back with him to our house in Deir Ghassanah. Traveling the mountain roads was extremely unsafe but it was the only way. They returned with us and the baby Majid, who was still in swaddling bands; whenever he wanted to be fed, we would pause under a tree so that my mother could give him a few gulps from her breast, waiting minutes that seemed longer than they really were because of our fear of ambushes, shelling, and the other surprises of the road.

I've never in my life seen a hyena, a wolf, or a jackal, but terror at the thought that they might appear on the road as we fled from Lydda to Deir Ghassanah brought them to life before my eyes. I've seen scorpions and vipers but never feared them as much as I did those creatures of my imagination. A child's facts are his fears, not objective facts. On that journey, I became aware that I was involved in something beyond my power as a child to understand. In fact, now, at the moment of writing, I discover that I can't remember its details.

Later, the Palestinians would develop a collective memory as precise as any individual's, as though whatever had touched one of them had touched them all. I asked my mother and she tells me that the passing of a bus or a car was a temporary lifebelt. We would get on without asking where it was heading and it didn't matter if it carried us one kilometer or took us to a village we didn't know. What mattered was that it take us away, or even that we should have the chance to sit for a while. I urge my mother to remember. Memory refuses to come to her aid but the phrase 'they betrayed us' repeats itself an amazing number of times in the course of her few sentences. From her sporadic words, I piece together the atmosphere of that sad exodus. Anxiety over what people had left behind and anxiety over what lay ahead. A world vanishing and another forming in its place beyond the control of the displaced. Everything that was known making way for everything that was unknown. Self-respect taking a back seat to necessity. Only necessity.

A father, a mother carrying a baby, and two small boys—Mounif, aged seven, and me, aged four. We walked inside fear itself toward the village that we thought of as our solution. At the time, we didn't know we were merely a tiny detail in a scene from the Nakba that befell the entire Palestinian people.

Thereafter Palestinian migrations would diversify, stretching from the coast to the mountains, from Palestine to abroad, and from one country to another, bringing the wandering in the wilderness full circle. The worst of these migrations was that of our fathers to the Gulf states, where money was plentiful. Some (I do not say all) of these produced the youth of that lost generation that received an upbringing based on affluence and a day-by-day and year-after-year fading of the memory of Palestine. Some of this generation have become used to taking and are no longer able to give. They behave as though their prosperity in the Gulf states is a natural thing that will last forever. They enter universities not by virtue of their superior academic performance and high scores but by virtue of their family's money. The student insists from first year onward on having a car and doesn't care who pays for it or covers its running costs so long as it isn't him. His clothes are flashy and all are the world's top brands. He spends half his time watching American TV series and going with his friends to parties, for a reason or for none. He has never in his life taken part in a demonstration to protest against anything and makes fun of anyone who has or who shows interest in any public issue. A generation that may poison the lives of its families in defense of its personal freedom but doesn't know what to do with that freedom or why exactly it wants it. The employment of millions of Palestinians in the Gulf may constitute another way in which the Arab system funds the Occupation and covers its costs with Arab money. The opening of the Gulf's doors was a boon to the Palestinians in the short term, in the years of refuge and migration that followed the Nakba, but in the long term it has certainly been less beneficial. Let me pause here and confess that I'm not completely sure of what I'm saying. The subject hasn't been studied yet with sufficient care. The Gulf provided many with a psychological and economic security umbrella without which it's impossible to imagine that people could have survived in the aftermath of the Nakba. Certain Palestinian organizations and parties were born or developed in the countries of the Gulf. Their assistance to the villages and their generous financial donations in aid of their relatives in Palestine had a role in reinforcing their continued presence on the land and in withstanding the pressures of the Occupation.

Later, at the time of the Six Day War, Mounif will be working in Doha, I will be a student in Cairo, Majid will be at the University of Jordan, and 'Alaa will be with my father and mother and attending primary school in Ramallah.

Majid decides to infiltrate on foot into Ramallah. He actually carries out his plan but is obliged to return to his studies a few days later. Since that visit, he hasn't seen the city. The family ties that link us are totally at odds with our geographical dispersal around the world. We can no longer tell which of us is the one who cares most about these ties but we all recognize that everyone needs everyone else and that no one is happy with his forced separation from the others, whatever the reason—study, work, or the Occupation.

I'll never forget something that 'Alaa, whose job as an engineer forced him to live for many years in Qatar, once said. We were all grown up and had been dispersed among many countries. In his summer vacation, which isn't more than one month a year, 'Alaa returns to Amman and lives in bliss at being back among the family again. Once, when the time came for him to return to his job and I went with him to the airport to say goodbye, he surprised me by saying, "I've started to hate love."

He said a great deal about the constant anxiety he felt over his mother when he is there and about his having to be separated from everyone to earn a crust of bread and educate his children and unburdened himself to me at length, but I remain amazed at the poetry sleeping in his amazing expression, "I've started to hate love."

Majid is a poet faithful to poetry but not desperate to publish his work in books. He issued his first verse collection after fifty years or a little less of continuous writing and erasing and is now preparing his second for publication. Ghassan, who introduced me to the electronic paradise through his skill at everything to do with computers, has built websites for Radwa, Tamim, and me and taught me how to edit mine—a true test of his patience and perseverance. The internet has rescued Majid particularly from his reluctance to write and publish and he has started doing so electronically and spending long hours in front of the computer, as though to make up for lost time. 'Alaa has taught himself to play the oud and started to write poems and songs that he sets to music himself.

Once Majid was done with the expatriates' conference, we all went together to Deir Ghassanah so that he could see it after his long absence.

My uncle's wife gave us the best possible reception. Our first lunch had to be musakhan, of course. The strange thing is that Marwan al-Barghouti phoned me too, by coincidence, and wanted to meet me. I suggested that he join us at Dar Ra'd, which he did, once again over Umm Talal's musakhan. This time I discovered that his family and my uncle's wife's family were related, though I failed to grasp exactly how, even after a long explanation.

As we left Dar Ra'd for the Alhambra, I was surprised to hear my mother make the following announcement: "I have decided to restore and modernize your uncle 'Ata's house and I shall build a new house for you all in the courtyard of Dar Ra'd. Mourid and Tamim now have identity cards and God willing the others will be able to claim the family reunion permit, so Dar Ra'd won't be big enough for everyone. Also, I've decided to buy al-Zawiya.'"

"What's al-Zawiya?"

"It's a house that's fallen down and no one lives in, but my mother and I lived there for a while long ago, when I was a child, and I want it."

'Omar Dhib, to whom the lodge had come by inheritance, decided to give it to my mother as a present. She actually registered it in her name at the Palestinian Lands Department and felt that she had rescued her memory and her memories. A few weeks later, she returned bringing a construction plan for the new house that was to be built in the courtyard of Dar Ra'd.

"Who drew the plan, Mother?"

"I drew it."

She spread out a piece of paper that she took from her handbag and there was a plan of the house, down to the smallest detail.

I brought the municipal engineer, who studied the plan, authorized it with minor modifications, and signed it, and she obtained the necessary permissions from the municipality.

She took up residence in my uncle's house, where she started by adding a balcony and a spacious kitchen, which she asked me to photograph after the restoration to show my uncle and his family in Amman. My uncle will never be able to go to Deir Ghassanah but he wanted to redo his house in case one of his sons, daughters, or grandchildren should return to live there one day. Next she came to an agreement with the building workers, who started to dig the foundations for the new house, and its pillars started to rise. I would visit her every Friday and find her sometimes issuing instructions to the workers, at others making them lunch, and at all times offering them tea as they worked.

The sight brought me very mixed feelings since, to construct a new house in the courtyard of Dar Ra'd, my mother had to have the workers uproot the last two orange trees there. No power could turn my mother aside from the house-building project.

"You mean to say the poet of Deir Ghassanah shouldn't have a house there?"

179

She falls silent for a moment, waiting for my reaction, so I say nothing. She proceeds with her argument.

"You mean to say when your brothers come back they should stay in the village as guests? And your son and his children don't need a house in their own village?"

I'd look at the land after the disappearance of the orange trees, one inner voice blaming my mother, another arguing for an understanding of her insistence that we should have a house of our own in Deir Ghassanah. I recalled the great khudari fig tree that I'd been so quick to blame my uncle's wife for cutting down years ago, though later I'd come to understand her decision. Today here I was, watching as our new house drove the greenery from Dar Ra'd. My uncle's wife had expanded her portion of the house so that for many years now it hasn't had a real garden. She'd thought that those who had left would never come back, and now we were back. What my mother had done seemed to symbolize how tied in with pain this return was. Had I, who had been shaken to the core on my first return by the uprooting of the great fig tree, now colluded with my mother in the uprooting of the orange trees? Why was my difference with her a whisper and a hint and not a battle? Should I have stood up to her project with all my might? I hadn't done so. Should I blame myself or my mother or a set of circumstances none of us would have suffered had not the hand of history turned the lives of every individual, family, and household in Palestine upside down? Wasn't it possible for us to be overcome by joy without that joy being overcome by sadness?

Were we obliged to choose between the tree that lifts the spirits and the roof that shelters?

Was that how things were—the beautiful or the necessary? The tree or the roof?

Is it freedom or disobedience to differ openly with your mother?

How often have I said that life resists simplification? Here it was, resisting again, for the thousandth time. I admired my mother's determination and her capacity for taking decisions and her initiative and I was upset at the disappearance of the two orange trees. Soon, though, this ambiguity ceased to be important.

The new building was finished in seven months. She slaughtered a sheep in celebration. She decided to call it 'Lightning and Ra'd,' after the name Ra'd, which means 'thunder.' She put a little furniture in it, gave me copies of the keys, and returned to Amman, intending to come back to furnish it and get it ready to be lived in. Then I could move there on a permanent basis, for I, being the only one of my brothers who had obtained the Palestinian identity card, was the only one who had the right to go to Deir Ghassanah.

Her plans would have succeeded, but for a small development that has prevented her from seeing the house to this day. Sharon took power in Israel after his visit to the al-Aqsa Mosque. The Intifada erupted; he imposed a siege on the Bank and Gaza and on Arafat's headquarters and closed the roads. The Israeli army set up the Surda checkpoint, cutting the road between Ramallah and thirty villages to the north, among them Deir Ghassanah. When, years later, things got a bit easier, my mother could no longer walk or travel because of the pains in her bones. She is obliged to stick to her seat next to the window in the Shmaysani house during the day, close to the heater, and to go to bed no later than nine. Because the default situation is closure and checkpoints and the exceptions are unreliable, the journey to the bridge and the uncertainties of the road have become unthinkable for her. The destiny of Umm Mounif's small new house is now tied to the ending of (at the least) the Middle East Crisis, the Arab-Israeli Conflict, and the War on Terror. At the least!

I think that one day I must clad its walls in old stone that looks like the stone of Dar Ra'd, so that I don't go on being sad at the eyesore of the cement. I inform my mother of my intention and she welcomes it straightaway.

But what of the nightmare of the foundation, its thievery, and its Namiqs?

It was clear from the first week that I was fighting a losing battle. I had to honor my contract for a full year. I got into lots of fights. Many people acted as mediators. It slowly dawned on me that each mediation was aimed, fundamentally and invariably, at guaranteeing the continuation of 'Namiqery.'

I got the message loud and clear early on.

All that remained was for me not to let my world be corrupted by that world.

I escaped into Greek myth. I read volumes, as though doing research, though I had no desire to do research; I just wanted to escape into a world other than the one I'd got caught up in. I started a long ode to Zeus and a poem called 'Hera.'

When I returned to Ramallah following my furious resignation, the bridge was packed, so it was night by the time I arrived. I went up to the Alhambra, turned the key in the lock, and entered. I pressed the light switch and before I could put my small suitcase on the floor, noticed something that pained me: most of the leaves of the Thai bush that I'd bought had fallen onto the red carpeting, making a perfect circle of dead leaves around the huge pot. I got the vacuum cleaner and cleaned the whole house but decided to leave the circle of dry leaves as it was. I don't know why I decided to leave it like that. My friends found the sight strange at first but got used to it. Dry leaves are time proclaiming its pre-eminence, death proclaiming its talent for victory. From one angle, I accepted it completely and from another I was play-ing the game of a realist who makes chivalrous acknowledgment of his opponent's strength. I am not alone in this room, then. Life isn't the only thing that lives here. Its opposite, its partner and murderer, known as death, shares its quarters, not as an honored guest but as a silent roommate whose presence is so quiet as to make him almost invisible. No one is aware of him, but these leaves that have turned completely dry point to his presence, which is something he neither intended nor is aware of.

I sat down next to the circle of dry leaves and wrote without pause until I had finished a poem that I called *Ghurfa mu'aqqata* (A Temporary Room).

Later, after many drafts and exclusions, I found that, without planning it, I had a collection of verse ready to be published.

The poems would set upon me like a highway bandit as I walked the roads of the world.

This is how the collection *al-Nas fi laylihim* (People at Night) was born, as well as more than half the collection *Zahr al-rumman* (The Pomegranate Flowers), which I published immediately after that.

As soon as 'The Pomegranate Flowers' appeared, I began writing *Muntasaf al-layl* (Midnight), a single book-length poem on which I spent more than two years.

Three collections one after the other. Then I stopped completely.

I stopped like someone returning from a marathon or who raises his hand in the dentist's chair as a signal that he can't put up with the sound of the drill any longer.

Was it the poetry that exhausted me or the pressures that made me write?

Or did I now need an overdue dose of laziness?

The amazing thing is that to be a poet you need two contradictory things—a great amount of vitality and a great amount of idleness. It's always easy to find the vitality because it's essential to staying alive. Any chance for idleness vanished with the invasion of Iraq.

History teaches us that political lies are a preface to war but the lies used to justify the invasion of Iraq exceeded all imagination and provoked millions of human beings on every continent. History has taught us that collusion among interested parties is widespread but the invasion of Iraq witnessed the collusion of governments at odds with their peoples and indifferent to the protests of millions of them, despite their high-flown talk of democracy. The invasion of Iraq upset the details of my daily life as much as the Occupation. American arrogance was now directed against every one of us and the era of universal apartheid between the strong and the weak began.

The worst thing about wars is that they reduce the enemy to a single characteristic. The country ceases to be history, language, architecture, theater, gardens, and legends; a heritage of love stories, philosophy, and science; shared ancestral dreams and uncountable varieties of human striving along the roads of the universe. Instead, every country becomes a mere label, blot, field of battle. This is what war has done to the names Palestine, Vietnam, Lebanon, Bosnia, Kosovo, Afghanistan, and Iraq. These are no longer multifaceted countries and their names are mentioned in news bulletins not as such but as 'fields'—fields from which the numbers of the dead and wounded are garnered daily like the output of a canned goods factory. The whole of history is now 'today' and today has become a reduction of every 'yesterday' that has passed over the face of this earth, a reduction of all history. As though al-Mutanabbi had never walked the markets of al-Kufa hugging himself with joy at a nation that would be singing his verses for a thousand years. As though the Abbasids had never built their libraries on the banks of the Tigris and Abu Nuwas never maintained his pinnacle of shamelessness and flagrant sexual indulgence through to the pinnacle of day after first exhausting the night with poetry and lovely depravities that spared neither male nor female. As though al-Hallaj had never been crucified defending what he had seen with the eye of the imagination and the eye of the mind. As though Hammurabi had never written his code on tablets of burnt clay before Coca-Cola and McDonald's had been transformed into a religion for all mankind, while Gilgamesh, who achieved immortality by *not* finding the plant of immortality on the steppes of his everlasting legend, is treated as though he were not of the land of Iraq. Bush and Rumsfeld reduced all this to the word 'enemy.'

Not one rational Arab believed for an instant that the Ba'th Party was synonymous with Iraq and not one believed that Osama bin Laden was synonymous with Islam. However, war wants to summarize and abridge, not because the U.S. cannot understand but because it doesn't *want* to understand. A Brazilian journalist once asked me, "To what do you attribute the West's 'misunderstanding' of Islam?"

My answer was, "If a 'misunderstanding' serves the interests of certain people and helps them realize their goals, those people will *decide* to misunderstand. In such cases, the misunderstanding isn't an accident that can be corrected through knowledge, dialogue, or better information. It's a *deliberate choice*."

When the politicians of the West decide that Islam is a religion based on violence and murder, they adopt the definition used by Islam's own extremists. While claiming to fight it, the politicians of the West generalize the extremist definition. They encourage the naïve to believe the extremists' theories. Today, in our own countries, numerous groups of Muslims also practice a deliberate 'misunderstanding' of Islam. Ignorance of the truth, or the intentional ignoring or polluting of it, is not only a characteristic of the oppressor. The oppressed may also be ignorant, may they not? At a mourning ceremony, the women may be taken aback to find a strange woman, with no connection to the deceased and unknown to his family and relatives, bursting into the house without permission and launching into her 'lesson in religion' to the weeping and mourning women, describing the torments of the grave as though she'd been there like some news agency correspondent, seen every detail with her own eyes, and returned to tell the tale with an 'accuracy' that instills terror in the souls of her listeners. Hundreds of satellite TV stations have appointed themselves spokespersons for Islam, handing over hours of their transmission time to jurisprudents of the small screen and charlatans with fatwas that no rational person accepts so that they can proclaim their contempt for medicine, science, history, geography, and all the arts, from music, dance, song, and cinema to the theater. The governments that claim to be waging war on such persons in reality compete with them in an attempt to prove that they are no less pious or faithful.

Piety is not the characteristic for which the Barghoutis are best known, but most of the women of the family now wear the hijab, including two of the wives of my three brothers, as do some of their daughters. I condemn neither the wearing of hijab nor those who have decided to wear it. What I condemn is turning hijab into a registered trademark of faith and a litmus test of piety, righteousness, and good morals. Hijab is a form of dress and dress neither proves nor disproves anything. Niqab, though, is a criminal offence. Why? Because a woman wearing niqab, whose face cannot be seen, is the equivalent of a car moving through the streets without a number plate.

Later, Uncle 'Ata suffers a brain hemorrhage and two days before his death, the doctors will decide that he is living his last hours. His son and daughter came from the Gulf, and find him lashed to life by a support apparatus of wires and tubes, unconscious in the final coma.

I am taken aback to see his six daughters and his son's wife bring a huge black Toshiba tape recorder into the intensive care unit and make repeated and laborious attempts to stuff its earpieces into his ears so that he can listen to a recording of verses from the Qur'an in the hope that this will cure him. The important thing, though, is that the doctors, nurses, and administrators of the Shmaysani Hospital in Amman don't dare remove the Toshiba from the intensive care unit lest they be accused of being irreligious.

I say to the girls in a calm voice that almost choked me, "You're right. Thanks to this Toshiba, my uncle will wake from his coma, leave the intensive care unit, and immediately play in the World Cup" (it was 2006).

One of them (Amal, the cheerful, laughing, easy-to-get-along-with, good-hearted one, who lives in the Gulf) answers me, "Please, Mourid. You don't believe in these things but we do. Please please don't interfere."

I leave the room bemused.

Two days later Uncle 'Ata will depart this life, everyone will move out of the hospital to see to the funeral arrangements, and the Barghouti Family League will open its doors to receive mourners.

My nieces went to university, traveled, worked as teachers, and mixed with society. What led them to make this shift in their lives, in unison, as a group, and all in the same direction?

In this age of satellite television, the book is no longer for many a source of knowledge. The satellite channels have been taken over by preachers, missionaries, and professional fatwa-makers, and television has become the locus of truth. This is not enough, however, to explain the phenomenon. What is certain is that this social upheaval has become general in all Arab countries. No less strange is what happened to Radwa in a hospital in Cairo.

She needed a very simple surgical procedure, the kind they call a 'one-day operation.' The doctor suggested that she do it at the private hospital with which he worked.

She was starting to come round from the anesthetic as she left the operating room.

The nurse was pushing her cart down the corridor toward the room. Close to the threshold, Radwa gave a small cough.

Suddenly, her face started to swell.

Tamim and I could see her face swelling in front of our eyes. The doctor had left, so we called him back. When he arrived, the swelling had increased so much that her eyelids were pressed shut and her face had turned into a smooth round ball twice its normal size, making Radwa a completely different person. It was terrifying because she was at risk of asphyxiation and her lips were pressed tightly together. The doctor noticed our fear and tried to reassure us and we had to appear reassured in front of her so as to lessen her fear. The doctor gave her the necessary medicine and the swelling ceased and then started gradually to subside. The traces were completely gone within a few days of our bringing her home.

This unexpected complication meant that we had to stay at the hospital for four days. That was enough for me to discover that we were in a mosque, not a hospital. I open the door to the room to look for a nurse to help in an emergency and find dozens praying in the corridor. Unable to go anywhere, I am forced to go back inside the room and wait for the prayer to end. After a day or two, I discover that the worshipers are not only of the hospital's doctors and workers but include guards from the nearby buildings, shop owners, traffic police-men from the surrounding area, some bus drivers belonging to the German School close to the hospital, and visitors and family members of patients. They drop everything for the prayer, and next to them their shoes are gathered, along with all the muck of the streets and roads outside that has stuck to them. I wonder, do the people in this corridor do this in order to demonstrate their 'faith' to one another? Is that why they don't pray in their own homes?

Given the situation, we should have been thinking exclusively about Radwa's well-being but the hospital had been transformed into a mosque, its doors blocked by bodies and mats, making it difficult to reach help in an emergency. The impossibility of asking for any emergency medical or nursing assistance from the hospital staff added further to our fears and worries. I still recall this provocative and intrusive situation with great perplexity and anger at what has become of our society.

Pains of social desiccation and times of barely opened, or almost closed, eyelids—and there is no enemy of the living creature more dangerous than desiccation, be it desiccation of the body, of the mind, of an idea, of a tree, of desire. I am speaking of the accumulation of 'historical pain' in our country—a pain that chases away peace of mind, logic, responsibility, tranquility, imagination, truth . . . and poetry.

They say that constant pain acts as an incentive to writing but I don't believe such nonsense. Pain sometimes acts as an impediment to writing. I consider myself a poet in decline, near the end of his run, and admire those who publish forty or fifty collections of verse on the grounds that their suffering is never-ending. Historical pain is a burden on the poem because its constant presence means that it's chronic, and all that is chronic, from inflammation of lungs to inflammation of rhymes, is boring. Palestinian pain due to the Occupation and Arab pain due to dictatorship have reached a point that disables poetry. What they call 'nationalist' poetry generally depends on rhetoric and eloquence. Eloquence may shake history but it doesn't protect geography.

Real pain doesn't need our rhetoric. In my collection *Mantiq al-ka'inat* (The Logic of Beings), I wrote the following very short poem to affirm this, to myself above all:

Truth needs no eloquence.
After the death of the horseman,
the homebound horse
says everything
without saying anything.

We have been living with 'chronic pain' and 'chronic resistance' for more than a century. The poets of the world wrote resistance poetry for a year or two and then went back to the poetry of ordinary life. How many years must people resist and how many years must their poets write resistance poetry? The French Resistance lasted for no more than four or five years, after which Aragon, Éluard, and the others returned to their experimentalism and the aesthetic playfulness that suited their temperaments. There aren't many cases of a people resisting for a whole century, and from the time that the fingernails of the Zionist movement started rapping on our windows until now, when they have pulled our homeland down around our ears, we've seen everything a poet or prose writer can imagine, to the point of satiety and vexation—every kind of death, every kind of patience, every kind of trying, and every kind of leader (except for one who can deliver, for whom we are still waiting, though that wait too has brought us to the brink of boredom). We've seen both despair and hope so often that we no longer know exactly what either of them is. We've seen pessimism, we've seen optimism, we've seen pessoptimism, and we've seen a whole line of United States presidents, so what is there left for us to see?

We've seen the seller of colored beads, the seller of poisons, the seller of dreams, the seller of delusions, the one who sells his party and the one who sells himself; the coward who flees the field and the brave man from whom the field flees; the tender and the cruel, the honest man and the liar, the sage and the idiot. We've seen those who

can distinguish fifty kinds of wine and those who wipe their noses on
their sleeves, so what is left for us to see?

We've seen smart bombs and stupid bombs, cluster bombs and
phosphorus bombs, fragmentation grenades, tanks, armored cars, bulldozers, secret agents, and silencers, so what is left for us see?

We've seen the detention camps of twenty Arab states, so what is
left for us to see?

I haven't written a poem for three years because I don't want to
put a helmet on my poem's head. I don't want to work as a war correspondent. I don't want to work as a fireman. I don't want to work as
an ambulance. I don't want my verse to get used to living in graves. In
the poem "Midnight" is the following passage:

Here is Death,
wearing padlocks as pendants,
his well-trained hounds at his heels;
his eternal belt
stuffed full of addresses.
He gently lays you in his ebony trunk
with his dark clothes,
handkerchiefs, combs,
and huge toothbrush,
preparing you for a journey
to a place he knows and you do not.

Yet, with the ending of the rain,
you discover
Death has overlooked you!
In a fit of irresponsibility
he has left you to this life;
you realize it is others who have died.

They have gone
for reasons as obscure
as the sources of the winds,
or they have departed
shrouded in banners
where winds go to sleep.

And though you can't recall the details
your extravagant joy
now mellowed,
comes back again to you.
Slowly and slyly,
it has kept its charms for you alone,
as if it were a bolt of lightning that,
after seven years' fermenting in the skies,
descends to strike,
electrifying you
from head to toe
from left to right,
snatching away your scepter.
Though you sought to evade it,
It returns to strike you,
because,
but for the hundred aches and pains
nagging at your window,
like the beggars at the traffic lights,
you were born for joy.

Yes! We were created for joy. We were created to reduce pain and increase pleasure. Isn't man's struggle with nature and with tyrants and invaders a sign of that goal? Isn't our enchantment with love, kindness, justice, harmony, and freedom another?

We had got used to facing whatever we had to, as though the world would never add further hardship to hardship.

But on one of those typical Cairo springs that are not without foreboding, or dust kicked up by the burning khamasin winds, something that had never occurred to any of us was to happen.

10

The Dawn Visitor

When I was deported from Egypt in 1977, I told myself that this would be the last slap in the face I'd take from that regime. I set about trying to reorganize our family life using whatever means were available to me in exile.

I learned to appear 'strong' though my fragility was plain to any intelligent eye.

To appear to have no need of others though my need for a prop increased as the years passed.

To appear 'under control' like a stove burning quietly.

I asked myself if I'd fallen victim to a schizophrenia that hid the truth about myself from me even before hiding it from the world around me.

Was I now the Mourid I knew or had another Mourid formed inside me, at whose features I did not care to look?

One thing I was sure of: I would have to endure.

I am not a piece of music and I am not a play contemplating men's destinies on a darkened stage. I am a father, a husband, a man with a cause, a poet, a son, and an uncle. I'm an adult and I'm supposed to provide answers and not just questions. I got used to my expulsion from Egypt and made it old news. I walked the roads of the world turning that page and trying with all my might to forget it. Life, though, taught me that you have to be free in order to choose, or be confused, or decide, or demolish, or build, or forgive, or apologize, or accept, or refuse; likewise—and here's the rub—you have to be free in order to forget.

The world didn't let me be free so that I could forget.

When I imagined that I'd forgotten or that I'd learned to coexist with my forgetfulness, the Egyptian police took it upon themselves to remind me that this was a delusion.

Tamim left Cairo for Boston on 20 August 2001. Just twenty-one days later, on 11 September 2001, the Twin Towers were blown up. He was obliged to live in an atmosphere of persecution directed against Arabs and Muslims in the United States instead of experiencing its social, scientific, cultural, and literary environment. What helped him, however, was the political openness of Boston and of New England in general. It is a fact that must be acknowledged that he was not subjected to harassment during the entire period of his residence there and that it was, for him, a normal period, with a certain measure of tension that should not be exaggerated, during which he was able to pursue his studies, teach his students, and read for the comprehensive exam that would precede the research and writing phases of his dissertation.

He took the comprehensive exam, passed, and returned to Cairo to do his research. He would take his laptop in the mornings and go to the library of the American University in Cairo, located a few steps from our house in Shari' al-Falaki, and there he would spend most of his time, racing to obtain the greatest academic benefit in the shortest possible time.

This was early in 2003 and America's around-the-clock preparations for the invasion of Iraq were speeding up.

It seemed certain that Bush would launch his attack on Iraq within two or three days.

Egyptian opposition activists had agreed via the Internet and cell phones to go to Tahrir Square in the heart of the capital at noon on whatever day the offensive started in order to demonstrate against the war.

The U.S. and British embassies are located not far from Tahrir Square, as is the American University.

At the American University, on the morning of Thursday, 20 March, a small number of students were trying to come up with a way to let the others know that the shelling of Baghdad had in fact begun during the early hours of the morning, so as to get them out to demonstrate without waiting for the agreed-upon time.

They decided to set off the fire alarm.

Students and teachers rushed out of their classrooms to see what was going on. News of the war spread. They set off spontaneously for Tahrir Square and occupied it before the government could put its fortifications in place. A little later, the Cairo University students and waves of local citizens poured in. The government had lost control of the situation.

The Egyptian government spends millions of pounds to protect this particular square and only very rarely in recent history have the students of Cairo University been able to get to it, because the security forces close the university's gates on demonstrators and imprison them inside the campus, making it impossible for them to get out.

The government found that the square had fallen early, and to a threat from an unexpected direction. The students of the American University are mostly children of the ruling class or of the social elite that has the means to pay its fees, and in the estimation of the security apparatus nothing is to be feared from such people. The state went crazy.

Tamim returned from the demonstrations at night and said he expected to be arrested. He spent the night at another house and nothing untoward happened.

He returned the following day.

We became less cautious and he slept at home.

At dawn, five Egyptian security officials forced their way into our house.

Through the partly opened door, the figure of a man in civilian clothes could be seen.

"We want Tamim al-Barghouti and we want to search the house."

"Who are you?"

"State Security."

"Where's your permit?"

"Open the door immediately."

"I want to see the written permit. This is kidnapping."

When the first man heard us insist on seeing the permit, he took a step to the right, bringing into our field of vision the man standing directly behind him—a soldier wearing gleaming black body armor that gave him the appearance of a two-meter-tall metal bar and who looked as though he were about to set off for the battle front. His index finger was on the trigger of his weapon. He said nothing. He jerked his body one step to the left and another of his colleagues appeared behind him—a huge leaden twin, who didn't speak either and whose hand, like his companion's, was ready for anything.

"There's no reason to be alarmed. Just a couple of questions. We'll bring him back to you in an hour or so."

They're inviting him for 'a cup of coffee,' I told myself.

No matter the differences in terms and methods from one Arab country to another, such people are always gracious when inviting their prey to be their guests and they will always be bringing them back in an hour or so at the most. Men and women have spent decades in the cells of the Arab regimes without ever finishing that damned cup of coffee.

We got the message.

The message of fear or, rather, of intimidation.

In dictatorships, local industry's finest product—the best made, best packaged, hardest wearing, and most quickly delivered to the home—is fear.

Helpless, Radwa and I would watch them as they took Tamim down the building staircase, their guns pointed at his back.

Thuggish authority is the same, whether Arab or Israeli. Cruelty is cruelty and abuse abuse, whoever the perpetrator.

What hurts most is the lack of a clear legal mechanism for what follows the arrest.

They don't tell you where they've taken him. His place of detention remains unknown to you—such places are many and they are scattered throughout Cairo. All you can do is look through your telephone list for the name of someone influential who may be able to direct you.

As to what happens to him there, it's no different from what any foreign occupation would do to a citizen who had the miserable luck to fall into the hands of its security forces. Humiliation, slapping, torture with hot and cold water, being hung from the ceiling with your arms behind your head, electric shocks, and sleep deprivation. None of those things may actually be done to him, but fear that they will is used deliberately to bring about the desired effect.

The night before his arrest, we were with Edward Said and his wife Mariam at the house of our friend Huda Guindi in Zamalek. Edward was talking to Tamim about his dissertation, asking him about his professors at Boston University, and telling him what he knew about them.

The following morning, Edward and Mariam were on their way to a resort on the Red Sea coast for a holiday when Edward found out via a phone call from a friend what had happened. He phoned me in the utmost fury.

"What can I do? Tell me how I can help."

"No one can do anything, Edward. Things will take their course."

Tamim, who had been given his rights in Palestine, a country he didn't know, would lose them in Egypt, the only country he knew.

He was born in Cairo to an Egyptian mother and educated at Egyptian schools, from the Happy Home kindergarten to al-Hurriya School, to Cairo University, to the American University in Cairo, where he obtained his master's degree. On arresting him, along with hundreds of other students, the Egyptian security authorities would treat him as a foreigner and 'advise' him to leave the country, unlike the Egyptian students, who typically would spend a few weeks or months in the detention centers, after which they would be released. If a male Egyptian marries a woman from the furthest reaches of Eskimo Land, Egyptian law automatically grants her and her children Egyptian nationality. At the time, this same right was not granted to a female Egyptian who married a non-Egyptian.

Tamim was forced to leave Egypt.

What has stayed with me from this incident was my inability to protect my son.

In Marrakech, Morocco, I was to see with my own eyes the most painful example of a father who couldn't protect his son. When I was invited to read poetry in a number of Moroccan cities, I was accompanied by Jamal al-Durra, father of the martyred boy Muhammad al-Durra. I arrived at my hotel in Marrakech on time but Jamal al-Durra didn't come. He didn't come for two days after that. The Egyptian authorities had prevented his brother, who was coming by land from Gaza to accompany him, from entering Egypt to catch the Moroccan plane, which left from Cairo. Jamal cannot move on his own because his right side is packed full of bullets, some of which surgeons managed to remove and some of which remain in place. After repeated telephone calls, the Egyptian authorities allowed him to travel alone and transported his brother from the border post in the Gaza Strip directly to Cairo Airport, to make sure he didn't spend a single hour on Egyptian territory. To the Arab regimes, the Palestinian is simply a security file. He is dealt with by the interior ministries, not the foreign ministries, as though to give meaning to the secret motto embraced by the Arab States from the Atlantic to the Gulf: "We love Palestine and hate the Palestinians." That said, the Rafah crossing point on the Gaza-Egypt border is the ugliest embodiment of the ruthlessness of Egyptian official policy and the cruelty with which the regime treats the ordinary Palestinian citizen.

The Arab States are now living the third phase of occupation.

In the first phase, the Arab citizen lived under foreign occupation.

In the second, he was occupied by his local rulers acting as proxies for the foreigners.

And now he's living the phase of double occupation, which is simultaneously local and foreign.

What Jamal al-Durra told me of the criminal killing of his son Muhammad in his arms added nothing to the stupefaction I'd felt when watching the scene on satellite TV. However, the muscles of his face and the look in his eyes as he spoke of his inability to protect his young son will stay in my mind for a long time.

Jamal al-Durra added one thing that made the week I spent in his company in Morocco bearable. He told me that his wife was pregnant and that he would name the new baby Muhammad so that Israel would have to go on living with Muhammad al-Durra even after it had murdered him.

At the time, Jamal al-Durra seemed strong to me, but when his younger brother helped him to take off his shirt one morning while I waited in their room to go with them to a joint appointment, I saw that his right arm was attached to his shoulder by a thin remnant of skin. A sudden spasm of embarrassment passed over his face when he noticed that I'd seen. My embarrassment at myself will last for a long time.

It is a strange irony that of three prisons in which Egyptian security would hold Tamim during the three days of his imprisonment, one was al-Khalifa/Deportations, the same prison they put me in in 1977.

Tamim sleeps in my place in the same packed communal cell. He eats the wedge of processed cheese and the crust of stale bread that they gave me as nourishment for an entire day. He sleeps as I slept, on the cement floor without a bed, and maybe a murderer or smuggler or thief next to him voluntarily gives him a blanket as one of them once did me. He makes his shoes into a pillow beneath his head as I once did.

I, who am free today, feel exactly as though they are imprisoning me for a second time.

As though I had never left their first prison.

As though I were in a never-ending prison that refuses to acknowledge any final act.

As though the prison were my personal city. This time we will live in it and grow up in it together, my son and I.

I entered the seventh decade of my life having spent only a few days in prison, and those in an Arab country ruled by an Arab dictator, not in Israel. The idea of prison constantly intrigues me though. In the mind of the dictator, prison is abstraction, not detail; an idea, not actualities—an idea that requires no proof or evidence, a personal concept, like temperament or taste, that cannot be questioned. This prison is the source of his unshakable peace of mind. And because issuing an order to put people in prison is the one solution that doesn't need much intelligence, prison is the dictator's first, easiest, and surest solution. The dictator will not change his mind so long as he is on his throne. He will change it when he is somewhere else (in a different world, for example), not before. The dictator's throne is his opinion. The dictator squats on his opinion like a hen sitting on her eggs. He and his opinion carry out all the rituals of his day together, bathing, doing their morning exercises, eating, working, playing, and fucking one another. He takes his opinion with him to sleep the way he does his dog. The dictator is faithful to his opinion and his opinion is faithful to him. He and his opinion wake up at the same instant (note the coincidence!); it never leaves his side through the hours of the day and it never leaves his side through the hours of his rule, which are the hours of his life. If the dictator falls sick, or goes on holiday, or is afflicted with senile dementia, he leaves his opinion in the keeping of loyal followers, such as policemen, advisors, editors-in-chief, ministers of information, and former leftists who have seen the light after hesitation and cauterization and being beaten unconscious and hung from the ceiling. It is preferred that there be, alongside these, poets, novelists, and critics who have fought long and with tremendous courage in defense of their inalienable right to possess a flexible spine that enables them to bow, with dazzling ease, before the chamberlain of the dictator's palace. They have held strikes and sit-ins to be allowed to assume a position in his government, that same government that is known for its wholehearted dedication to the patronage of culture and the intelligentsia (just like that, with no expectation of reward!). The dictator has a sadistic love of obedience, rewarding the obedient by doubling his efforts to humiliate them, to the point that he uses them for his entertainment every time he sees them. The worst thing about a dictator, though, is his minor underlings.

When the time comes for Tamim's deportation, the deportations officer will allow me to accompany him. Two members of the security forces, charged with guarding him up to the last moment, ride with us. Near the end of the long, crowded, choking road to Cairo Airport, the driver, 'Abd al-'Al, gives me a word of advice: "Don't forget the tips, Mr. Mourid."

"The tips?"

"Yes, sir. The tips."

"For whom?"

"For them."

"Are you joking? Tips for the men deporting my son, 'Abd al-'Al?"

He whispers in my ear, "So that everything goes alright at the airport, sir. So they don't complicate matters."

"How much?"

"Whatever you think proper, sir."

"Fifty pounds? A hundred pounds?'

"Keep going, sir."

I pay the tips to the two men.

I am going to keep Tamim company on the plane to Amman. This time they allow Radwa to say goodbye to us, so she comes in another car with her friend Hasna Mekdashi.

The plane's front wheels rise and we are airborne. I feel as though I too am being deported and expelled a second time. I relive the day of my expulsion from Egypt in 1977 as though it still hadn't turned into the past. All the people in the airport's halls—the hundreds packing its front hall to say goodbye to their departing relatives, the dozens standing at the counter where the tickets are checked and the baggage weighed, the parallel rows for the passport stamping windows, the customers in the café in front of the gates leading to the boarding areas—all these are not here at the airport to say goodbye, travel, drink coffee and tea, or mount the steps to the departing aircraft; they are here to gaze at the iron shackle that links my wrist to that of the policeman accompanying me, who drags me through the halls before the eyes of all like a heavy suitcase.

This fat old woman will think I'm a thief. That teenage girl will think I raped a girl her own age. This customs officer with the dyed hair will think I'm a currency smuggler who has fallen into their hands as a result of brilliant planning, or an international criminal that Interpol has finally succeeded in catching after years on the run, and that now I'm being taken off under guard to suffer my punishment. A traveler in a hurry who treads on my foot by mistake and doesn't apologize will think I represent some kind of danger and that getting rid of me is a matter of urgency to him personally. It will never occur to them that I'm a poet whom authority, or the regime, is afraid of. So many of the country's intelligentsia and its important writers let the country—and the people—down that authority isn't afraid of them any more. People stopped reading poetry when poets deluded themselves into thinking that modernism meant gibberish. At the same time, they watched many literary icons colluding with the ruler. They did this in three ways: by desperately striving to obtain his approval; or, if that failed, by desperately striving to avoid his anger; or, if that failed, by quitting and migrating either to their inner worlds, which had been destroyed by melancholy, or to the world outside them, where they found themselves caught between the jaws of absence and of forgetfulness.

Certainly, everyone at the airport today will think I'm a criminal. No one will think I'm a poet who writes and rewrites a poem time after time until the poem is happy with its shape and I am happy too. I'm not a hero that I should feel pride, and I'm not a criminal that I should feel shame.

During these moments, I'm a person without feeling.

As though I were dreaming that I'm dreaming.

As though I weren't here, weren't with them, weren't with anyone, weren't coming from anywhere, weren't going anywhere. As though it were someone else they were taking away.

This was my state exactly as I fumed and almost exploded, though appearing before all those people as calm as an ironed shirt in a drawer full of clothes.

This was my state exactly as I wished I were a Greek god so that I could kick the blank walls of the airport with a sacred rope sandal and leave its high ceiling resting on nothing but the pillars of my curses.

On that day, when the past had still to become the past, the policeman took me up the stairs and all the way to my seat on the plane. Only there did he undo the shackles that linked my wrist to his, and leave.

I know what the others passengers thought as I came through the door of the plane in shackles. I know why the flight attendant switched the smile in which she'd been trained for so many months for a fearful look of suspicion and then averted her face. I know why, when she put the meal down in front of me, she did so as though she were a faceless prison guard thrusting a loaf at the prisoner through the aperture in his cell door. I know that people find it the more comfortable option to respect you if they see that someone else respects you and to despise you if they see that someone else despises you. But shouldn't a person make up his own mind? Shouldn't he examine the reasons to respect or despise you? I tell myself sometimes, especially when things are a little mixed up, that the brain is the laziest of the body's members and its dullest.

Alone, between sky and earth, I think of Radwa.

Radwa would pay for the policies of Sadat and his successor Mubarak in the coin of her own private life. She would experience the expulsion of her husband and dedicate her time to caring for her son without the presence of his father for seventeen years, except for short and intermittent periods. When she was obliged to undergo a life-threatening operation, she would be alone with Tamim, who was not yet three years old, while I was in Budapest and forbidden to put my mind at rest about her and be by her side. My mother flew to Cairo the moment she heard of the disease and that lightened the burden for me a little. Once more I had failed to be where I ought to be.

I fail to love, or show tenderness, or support, or help, or to look after, or be of use to those whom I love.

I had left Budapest for Doha to visit Mounif, Majid, and 'Alaa. While there, I got a telephone call from Radwa informing me that she had to have a major operation that couldn't wait.

What can the banished do to defeat a state, when their bodies are singled out as the target of its army, its police, its prisons, its borders, its stamps, and its 'sovereignty'? Whenever anyone tried to intercede with a senior Egyptian official to allow me to visit or to have my name removed from the blacklist at the airport, he was told, "It's a matter of sovereignty." Long live sovereignty!

If one could voluntarily decide to go mad, I would have decided to go mad.

It occurred to me that the lucky Arab is the one who wakes up one morning and finds that he's gone mad. That way it's all over.

I haven't gone mad.

Or has a thread of madness accompanied me till now, without my being aware of it?

I returned from Doha to Budapest stricken with silence. I turned the key in the door, sat down on the chair to rest for a few minutes before opening my suitcase, and woke up the next day still fully dressed. I went to work and found I couldn't stand the voices of my colleagues. Every time one of them opened his mouth, I wanted him to shut up. I asked for permission to leave.

That mood didn't last for more than a day.

I didn't realize at the time how much ground I had covered in terms of educating myself in getting used to things being disordered, in getting used to the fact that things were by their very nature disordered. The process had begun slowly and with difficulty in June 1967 and continued to firm up by degrees as I underwent all the other unpleasant personal shocks which, with time, had ceased to shock me, by which I mean that I became too dulled to collapse or grumble at my pains. I'd tell my friends jokingly, "Don't worry, guys. I'm not going to feel bad every time I'm supposed to. I'm not going to get sick every little while. I'm going to drop dead without warning."

The operation was successful but to this day Radwa's health remains generally delicate and this makes her susceptible to pains that she has learned to bear with a dazzling courage I'm incapable of learning from. If I catch so much as a passing runny nose I get into a panic and fill the world with my complaining and whining, and if my temperature goes up one degree I'm a dead man for sure (a business that deserves to be mocked and is apparently a bane of the male—but who among us can claim to have rid himself completely of the weaknesses of male nature that have come down to us through the generations?).

Did I say I'd fill the world with my complaining at every passing runny nose? Didn't I say in the paragraph before that I didn't feel bad or complain? Am I contradicting myself here? Yes! I'm contradicting myself and it amazes me that people are terrified of exposing their contradictions, flying off the handle in dismay at such an 'ugly' charge and defending themselves as vehemently as if their honor had been attacked. It doesn't scare me when someone yells in my face during a discussion, "But you're contradicting yourself, Mr. Mourid!" I reply "Of course I'm contradicting myself. You're right. That is indeed a contradiction." Sometimes I apologize for my contradictions and sometimes I don't. Humans are full of contradictions however much they deny it. Each of us holds within him contradictory voices to each of which he listens at different times, thus making his inconsistency clear for all to see. Nor do those who yell at me "You're wrong, Mr. Mourid" scare me. Of course I will sometimes be wrong. What's so strange about that? Am I so stupid as to always be right?

Radwa will suffer for years from an irritable colon and in Budapest she contracted acute pleural effusion, which is life-threatening. An aged Hungarian doctor, experienced and gentle, gives her treatment and she recovers once more. With her illness and her permanently delicate health, she seems to me to be made of glass that may break at the lightest touch and this terrifies me. Nevertheless, she confronts the challenges in her life with the hardness of a diamond. Throughout Tamim's childhood, she organized her university, political, social, and cultural calendars so as never to leave the house after seven in the evening. I was well aware that she was under threat not only of possible harm at a time when the two of them were alone but even of being arrested for her political stands. This was what she feared most, and it was impossible for her to predict how best to deal with the consequences should that happen. Phone calls weren't easy at that time. Letters sent by mail took a month or a little less (e-mail, chat rooms, and Messenger would have been something out of science fiction). In the slightly more distant past, when Radwa went to

Amherst in the United States in 1973 to obtain a doctoral degree, we had to wait more than a month before we could set up our first telephone call.

Our (recent) phone calls between Amman and Cairo continued with the aim of ensuring Tamim's return to Egypt. Meanwhile he occupied my spacious white office that looks out over the garden in Amman and sat down to write his famous poem "They Asked Me, Do You Love Egypt? I Said, I Don't Know." The intensity of the campaigns of support for Tamim in Egypt, the Arab world, and the rest of the world amazed me. His professors at Boston University sent letters expressing their dismay to the Egyptian government and a number of Arab writers had already done the same. In Egypt, solidarity with him extended to far wider circles. Thirty-four days after he was deported, we received confirmation from Radwa that the efforts had succeeded and that Tamim could return to Egypt, which he did.

How many journeys and how many returns, I ask you, Time? We seem to sink and bob back up with boring regularity. As though the dry land were waves that roll us over every time we take a step.

11

An Ending Leading to the Beginning?

On my last visit but one to Ramallah, I found my friends swapping stories of an incident at the luxurious Darna restaurant. When I asked my friend Ziyad about it he invited me to dinner there so that I could hear the details from its owner. The latter hugged me and said to Ziyad, "Leave him to me for a while." He took me upstairs, where he asked the waiter to bring him the photos. The waiter did so and my friend started showing them to me one by one. In all of them, the tables, chairs, plates, drawings, and glass of the elegant restaurant were smashed and bullet holes were visible in its columns, walls, ceiling, stairs, door, and floor. He told me the story in detail: "A number of armed fighters belonging to Fatah had become so fed up and angry at the widely known corruption of the Authority's men that they decided to launch an armed attack on the Authority's headquarters to express their fury. Of course, at the gate to the president's headquarters at al-Muqata'a, they came up against their comrades-in-arms of the duty guard, who were no less angry than the attackers but told them, 'You won't find the ones you're looking for here. Go look for them in the most luxurious hotels and restaurants, where they spend each evening.'"

The angry Fatah men turned around with their weapons and made the Darna restaurant their starting point.

They burst into the restaurant through the main door and started shooting at random.

They didn't intend to kill but to use the bullets as a final scream of protest. They intended to proclaim their fury at the leadership, the exhaustion of their patience, and their despair at all the promises of reform that had gone unrealized down the years. The customers hid themselves under the tables, of course. I saw a photo of one of them reaching up with his hand to the top of the table from underneath in spite of all the bullets so that he could grope for his glass, in which there was still a little beer, and I laughed.

Corruption is reaching a crisis point. The violence of the Occupation is increasing. Fatah is falling apart. Hamas is rising. This proves that the abyss can widen to take two victims at one time when both lose their minds.

The Authority has decided to sit on its throne waiting for the Israeli tank to smile.

The tank doesn't smile.

The Arab rulers behave as though their countries are in a dilemma that can be resolved only by making concessions to their enemy and thus defusing the danger he represents. It never occurs to them that it is the Zionist project that is in crisis and that today it is caught in a real dilemma, which it doesn't know how to get out of.

The Palestinian people, on whose disappearance it based all its calculations, haven't disappeared and are still here, in its singular hell known as 'the Occupied Homeland.' In addition, Israel hasn't won a clear victory in any of its confrontations with the Arabs since 1967. Despite this, the Arab leaders have yet to lose their fear of victory. Indeed, they rejected victory when they clearly achieved it in 2006 in southern Lebanon and claimed defeat, so attached were they to the latter. The 'peace process,' on whose pillow they have been sleeping so long, has exploded under all their heads. It's just not working, chaps! The absurd peace process has killed more Arabs than all of Israel's wars together. More dangerously than all this, though, it has seduced the Arab leaders into highjacking the meaning of the Palestinian cause itself and transforming it from one of national liberation into an NGO, and from a program of resistance into one of assistance, ignoring in so doing something every citizen knows, which is that the only form of resistance the Israelis will allow the Palestinians is the presentation of bunches of flowers to the soldiers of the Occupation. However, there aren't enough flowers in Palestine for an army that keeps up its good work with such energy and constant appetite. During the long siege that the government of Israel has imposed on Gaza, tons of Gazan flowers prepared for export to Europe have become free food for sheep and goats, which munch on them with relish on Valentine's Day. The Israeli army conducts its maneuvers against our bodies, and with live ammunition. Every time, it 'keeps trying what's already been tried' and doesn't calm down and doesn't relax and doesn't solve its security problem. Israel has tried every kind of military assault against the Palestinians. The United States and the governments of Europe have tried every door except the one door that would lead to a real chance of a solution, which is the door of justice.

Palestinian official impotence, however, isn't our last word. Here is a people that has never ceased to be extraordinarily creative in coming up with ways to go on living. What is new is that it is now clear that the Namiqs will never liberate the land and that the Palestinians must do something to reclaim their cause, which has been highjacked by political corruption. They must repossess the moral significance of resistance, cling to its legitimacy, and rid it of the bane of constant improvisation, chaos, and ugliness. The oppressed wins only if he is essentially more beautiful than his oppressor.

How much time has been lost?

The Palestinian cause is starting over again from the beginning. Wasn't the beginning that a land was occupied and has to be reclaimed? And that a people was expelled from its land and has to return? Is the end that we have come to today anything other than that beginning?

Glossary

the Green Line: the demarcation lines set out in the 1949 Armistice Agreements between Israel and its neighbors (Egypt, Jordan, Lebanon, and Syria) after the 1948 Arab–Israeli War. The Green Line is also used to mark the line between Israel and the territories captured in the Six Day War, including the West Bank, Gaza Strip, and Golan Heights. The name alludes to the green ink used to draw these lines on the maps during the armistice talks.

Hanthala: a cartoon character (named after colocynth, a bitter-tasting plant) created by Naji al-ʻAli; a Palestinian Everyman.

kanafeh: a dessert made of vermicelli-like pastry filled with soft cheese and drenched with syrup.

khamasin: the period of approximately fifty days in spring in Egypt during which oppressively hot dust-laden winds often blow.

kufiya: a square of cloth folded and worn over or wrapped around the head by Palestinian men.

the Muqataʻa: the administrative center of the Palestine National Authority, in Ramallah. It and its occupants, including President

Yasser Arafat, were besieged by Israeli armed forces from March to May 2002.

musakhan: a Palestinian dish of chicken, bedded in onions, basted in olive oil, smothered with sumac, and oven-roasted on flat bread.

the Nakba: 'the Catastrophe,' referring to the expulsion of the Palestinians from their homeland and the establishment in it of the State of Israel in 1948.

rababa: a folk instrument consisting of a sound box, long neck, and strings, played with a bow.

sandawitshat: sandwiches (a term taken from English and widely used).

shata'ir: sandwiches (a term coined by the Arabic Language Academy to replace sandawitshat).

The Suspended Odes: seven poems by the greatest poets of pre-Islamic Arabia, which were engraved on plates of gold and suspended in the Kaaba at Mecca before the coming of Islam. They remain among the most highly regarded works of Arabic literature.

A NOTE ON THE AUTHOR

Mourid Barghouti was born in 1944 near Ramallah. He has published thirteen books of poetry in Arabic including a Collected Works (1997) and received the Palestine Award for Poetry in 2000. His memoir *I Saw Ramallah* was published in English in Cairo in 2000 and by Bloomsbury in 2004. A selection of his poetry, *Midnight and Other Poems*, was published in English in 2008. He lives in Cairo with his wife, the novelist and critic Radwa Ashour.

A NOTE ON THE TRANSLATOR

Humphrey Davies has translated many Arabic books by a wide range of authors including Bahaa Taher, Khaled Al-Berry, Muhammad Mustagab, Yusuf al-Shirbini, Gamal al-Ghitani and Ahmed Alaydi. His translation of Elias Khoury's *Gate of the Sun* was awarded the Banipal Prize, and that of Alaa Al Aswany's *The Yacoubian Building* was voted Best Translation of 2007 by the Society of Authors.

A NOTE ON THE TYPE

This book is set in 11-point Times New Roman, with a display font of 33-point Linotype Didot.